D0070587

THE
BLOODY
FLAG

Post-Communist Nationalism in Eastern Europe

Spotlight on Romania

SP PC SOCIAL PHILOSOPHY & POLICY CENTER

THE BLOODY FLAG

Post-Communist Nationalism in Eastern Europe

Spotlight on Romania

Juliana Geran Pilon

with a foreword by Robert Conquest

transaction

Transaction Publishers
New Brunswick (USA) and London (UK)

Published by the Social Philosophy and Policy Center and by Transaction
Publishers 1992

Library of Congress Cataloging-in-Publication Data

Pilon, Juliana Geran.
    The bloody flag : post-communist nationalism in eastern
  Europe : spotlight on Romania / Juliana Geran Pilon, with a foreword
  by Robert Conquest.
      p.   cm. — (Studies in social philosophy & policy : no. 16)
      Includes bibliographical references and index.
      ISBN 1-56000-062-7 (cloth) — ISBN 1-56000-620-X (pbk.)
      1. Nationalism—Romania—History—20th century.
  2. Nationalism—Europe, Eastern—History—20th century.
  3. Romania—History—1989- 4. Europe, Eastern—History—1989-
  5. Nationalism. I. Title. II. Series.
  DR268.P55   1992
  949.8—dc20   92-1310
                                                    CIP

Cover Design: Kent Lytle

I dedicate this book to my parents, Charlotte and Peter Geran,
who taught me the importance of tolerance,
generosity, and a sense of humor.

Series Editor: Ellen Frankel Paul
Series Managing Editor: Harry Dolan

The Social Philosophy and Policy Center, founded in 1981, is an interdisciplinary research institution whose principal mission is the examination of public policy issues from a philosophical perspective. In pursuit of this objective, the Center supports the work of scholars in the fields of political science, philosophy, law, and economics. In addition to this book series, the Center hosts scholarly conferences and edits an interdisciplinary professional journal, *Social Philosophy & Policy*. For further information on the Center, write to: Social Philosophy and Policy Center, Bowling Green State University, Bowling Green, OH 43403.

Contents

Acknowledgments

I wish to thank the Earhart Foundation and in particular its president, David Kennedy, for awarding me a fellowship that made this book possible. And I am grateful to Richard W. Soudriette, Director of the International Foundation for Electoral Systems, for offering me the opportunity to be involved in the process of democratization that is taking place in post-Communist Eastern Europe.

I also wish to thank the National Forum Foundation and its president, Jim Denton, for affording me the possibility to meet many of the brightest and most effective young leaders of East-Central Europe during their NFF internships. Among them have been the writer Mirces Mihaesi of the Timisoara Society; Ion Bogdan Lefter and Cristian Moraru, both of *Contrapunct*; and many others.

Other Romanians who have helped me understand the situation in the country include: Nicolae Manolescu, editor of *Romania Literara* and chairman of the Civic Alliance party; human-rights activist Smaranda Enache; Vasile Gogea, philosopher and a founder of the "November 15 Society" in Brasov; Daniel Popescu, president of the Students' League; and a great many others.

I also have many friends in the United States who have assisted me with the study: Professor Vladimir Tismaneanu, Associate Director of the Center for the Study of Post-Communist

Societies at the University of Maryland; poet Dorin Tudoran, editor of *Agora* and *Meridian*; Professor Leonard Liggio, Senior Scholar at the Institute for Humane Studies; Steve Miller, editor of *Soviet/East European Report*; Paula Dobriansky, Associate Director for Programs at the U.S. Information Agency; and many others.

Above all, I am deeply indebted to my husband, Roger Pilon, Director of the Center for Constitutional Studies at the Cato Institute, for elucidating many of the principles at the root of a liberal society, and to our children, Alexander, six, and Danielle, twelve, for being patient while I was immersed in study and writing.

Finally, many thanks are due to Ellen Frankel Paul, Deputy Director of the Social Philosophy and Policy Center, for her advice and encouragement in the writing of this book, and to Harry Dolan, the Center's Managing Editor, for an excellent job of editing.

Foreword

Juliana Geran Pilon's book on present-day nationalism in Eastern Europe is as penetrating as it is wide-ranging. It presents the philosophical and the historical basis for nationalism in general, for the specific types of nationalism to be seen in the area, and also for the characteristics they have in common.

The very dangerous possibilities which such nationalism may provoke are clear enough today in the Yugoslav case; and serious analysis—of which there is anyhow too little found in the West—is to be welcomed. A particular strength of Dr. Pilon's work is her analysis of the relationship between Communism and nationalism.

Her spotlight on Romania is particularly welcome. After 1946, that country developed all the worst characteristics of Communism and nationalism, in a sort of general totalitarian schema. Moreover, attention to Romania is particularly apt at present: for the Romanian government and ruling caste are the only ones in Eastern Europe which have not been removed by democratic revolution, but which have worked hard to give the opposite impression—even deceiving many in the West, for whom the realities need to be firmly deployed.

We must all be grateful to Dr. Pilon for her broad and stimulating contribution to the literature.

Robert Conquest

Introduction

The collapse of the Soviet empire, exhilarating as it may be for geopolitical reasons, as well as encouraging to the people of the captive nations who may now realistically hope for a freer life, brings with it serious aftershocks. The legacy of nearly five decades of Communist rule is no small problem: a tortured populace, silenced and famished, subjected to lies and complete political control, has emerged traumatized and tired.

Perhaps the most urgent need before the people who have recently undergone a change of regime, no matter how incomplete, as in Romania, is the need to carve out an identity. A sense of purpose and self-definition is almost as basic as nourishment. This is one of the main reasons for the need to properly understand—not simply, and simplistically, condemn—post-Communist nationalism. If it can be attained, an honest self-definition may well provide a healthy sense of self-worth and renewed confidence. Equipped with an instrument of continuity to their past and their rich—if sometimes checkered—traditions, there is hope that the nations of Eastern and Central Europe will be able to breathe, survive, and create once more.

The danger, however, is that instead of a healthy reappraisal of those traditions—including a sober and critical assessment of the dark moments of intolerance and ignorance—there will be

1

jingoism and an inability to either forgive or move on to another historical level. Specifically, there is a chance that the intrinsic pathology of the past half-century will be deliberately exploited by the defeated elite—the *nomenklatura*—in cooperation with delinquent, chauvinistic fringe elements in these nations, to create a lethal, self-destructive, one might say even auto-cannibalistic implosion. The only effect of a hate-filled, racist, and xenophobic nationalism is the disappearance of any hope for democracy and the rise of a different (yet not necessarily less dangerous) authoritarianism than the recently defeated Marxist variety. If one may speak in images, the red flag of the Communist revolution risks turning into the bloody flag of nationalism.

The magnitude of the danger is revealed each passing day. Writes Vladimir Tismaneanu, the foremost American student of Romania's Communist history:

> One of the prevailing illusions during the post-communist euphoric stage was that xenophobia and other outbursts of the tribalist, pseudo-communitarian, and mystical-romantic spirit would remain merely a marginal phenomenon. As the economic situation has continued to deteriorate and the new elites have failed to offer persuasive models for a rapid transition, those movements have gained momentum. They have recruited primarily among the frustrated and disenchanted social groups by stirring responsive chords among those unable to overcome the traumatic effects of a sudden break with the past.[1]

The result is intolerance, exclusiveness, nostalgic images of a past that never was, and a resurgence of anti-liberalism. Tismaneanu sees this as a conflict "less between communists and anti-communists than between collectivism and liberalism"—which may yet spell dictatorship, and chaos.

Yet this brief study is inspired by the conviction that a nation can be both liberal—in the classical sense, that is, respecting the individual and his voluntary associations—as well as national, indeed, multinational. The case of the United States, at once the most powerful and most advanced modern pluralist, multi-ethnic state in the world, stands by way of promising example that such an ideal is not unrealistic but, on the contrary, presents the most pragmatic, most economically successful, and—above all —most eminently moral of political models. This is not to say that it is perfect; far from it. But it has done well, and its classical-liberal model is worth emulating.

At the same time, it is impossible to deny that retrieving, or perhaps more accurately "creating anew," a meaningful sense of national identity in Eastern and Central Europe is a crucial task. But it is also nearly insuperable, its difficulty and delicacy not to be underestimated. For at bottom nationalism is "irrational"—in the precise sense of being extra-rational. Isaiah Berlin, for example, offers a clinical, pathological assessment: "Nationalism is an inflamed condition of national consciousness which can be, and has on occasion been, tolerant and peaceful. It usually seems to be caused by wounds, some sort of collective humiliation."[2] Yet such is the power of reason that it can assist the other faculties. If we analyze the different logical components of nationalism, my hope is that a balanced concept may yet emerge, and unnecessary convulsions, including even bloodshed, may be avoided.

It would be easy to dismiss nationalism as just another aberration steeped in nineteenth-century romanticism, an evil spirit, chauvinism with a thin veneer of ideological respectability. There are even those who deplore the demise of Communism, which is being credited, so the argument goes, with having "kept the lid on" nationalist feelings. While there is certainly some truth to this—since Communism kept the lid on most of the captive people's feelings—there is no point in denying the real issues, colored by modernism, secularism, and a *fin de siècle* malaise, relating to man's place in history and society.

The term "nationalism" is neither simple nor unequivocal. Gale Stokes is correct when he says that it "is not primarily captured in class relations, and is not reducible primarily to social relations, but is rather a complex ideology, with all the overtones of state apparatuses, cultural systems, and social interactions that word currently implies"[3] in the popular mind.

The rich scholarship that deals with the concept of nationalism[4] deserves renewed consideration in the context of the traumatized East-Central European nations that are currently beginning to reach back to civilization and reconstruct their own traditions in a manner that will allow them to face themselves, to come to grips with the years of mendacity, and to acquire the self-confidence to embark on a new road toward a genuine civil society.

I chose to focus special attention on Romania because in many ways it represents a worst-case scenario in East-Central Europe, with the obvious—and somewhat idiosyncratic—exception of Yugoslavia. Having experienced serious pre-Communist upheavals, Romania's democratic institutions were obliterated at the time of the Soviet takeover in August 1944. But then came the real deluge: Romania was subjected to a continuously ruthless and particularly perverse form of Communism, under Gheorghe Gheorghiu-Dej and Nicolae Ceausescu respectively. The country's uniqueness is linked both to the weakness of the pre-Communist nationalist left and the strength of nationalism during the interwar period, including a significant fascist influence.

The revolution of 1989, moreover, did not put an end to the Communist regime in Romania; rather, the revolt coincided with a "palace coup" which quickly succeeded in "hijacking" the revolution and putting an end to its high hopes for systemic overhaul. Thus, while currently undergoing privatization—or at least some version of it—the country continues to be ruled by members of the old regime whose commitment to democracy is questionable at best. Meanwhile, the dissident opposition—

surprisingly well-organized in light of its recent conception—is still embryonic.

The country's ethnic minorities are sizeable, making up nearly 12 percent of Romania's population. They are Hungarians (the largest group, constituting some 7.9 percent of the population), Germans, Serbs, Ukrainians, Gypsies, and others. The large Hungarian population is also relatively mature politically and is determined to preserve its cultural identity after the traumatic experience of Communist uniformism. The Jewish population has dwindled to a negligible number—about eighteen thousand from over eight hundred thousand before the Second World War—as a result of deportations and murders during the war and massive emigration since then. Numbers aside, their cultural presence has outlived them, and the East-Central European phenomenon of "anti-Semitism without Jews" is alive and well.

The reality of anti-Semitism is in fact a microcosm of the problem at hand. Writes Henry Kamm in *The New York Times* of June 17, 1991: "Jews and other Romanians, as well as foreign diplomats, venture various guesses at the motivation for the growing anti-Semitism. Most cite the general rise of nationalism, of which slander against Jews is a classical component. . . . Others note that Jews, as well as ethnic Hungarians, were prominent among the early Communists, whom Moscow installed in power in 1944." Hence a mixture of ethnic, ideological, and geopolitical considerations all play a part in the complex of attitudes toward Jews and other minorities in Romania.

In brief, the Romanian situation is interesting and critical: the Romanian majority needs to come to grips with its national definition while seeking both greater freedom for itself and peaceful ways of cohabiting with others in a situation that is still explosive and is likely to continue to be so for the foreseeable future. Yet the problem of an emerging nationalism is endemic to all of East-Central Europe in the aftermath of Communism. My hope is that some of the conceptual tools developed in the context of Romania will be of help to others in the region and to Western analysts attempting to understand this tumultuous area of the world.

The present study will analyze the issue of nationalism in four chapters. The first chapter, "Some Basic Philosophical Categories," consists of four sections, each of which defines different components of nationalism: the cultural aspects of a nation's experience; the political aspects of national integrity; metaphysical definitions of ethnicity; and aggression or struggle for power disguised as nationalism. The approach is mainly philosophical but with historical illustrations, in order to outline several important conceptual categories by making reference to some classic works on the subject. Chapter II focuses on the case of East-Central Europe, with specific reference to its post-Communist trauma in a historic context, while Chapter III discusses only Romania. Chapter IV, "Some Notes on Harmony," explores some possible classical-liberal solutions, specifically citing the work of Austrian economist and philosopher Ludwig von Mises, whose commitment to individualism was coupled with a strong endorsement of nationalism and ethnicity.

The afterword, "Subterranean Societies," is a penetrating reflection on nationalism by a Romanian revolutionary, Vasile Popovici, who teaches French literature at the Timisoara University and is the founder of the anti-Communist Timisoara Society. Finally, the appendix cites and briefly discusses the section on national minorities from the Copenhagen Document of the Conference on Security and Cooperation in Europe.

I

Some Basic Philosophical Categories

1. Cultural Aspects of a Nation's Experience

When man first realized that his stay on earth is brief and precious, he must have deplored the predicament yet simultaneously sensed a need to celebrate his life: thus culture, and "beauty" variously defined, came forth. Language—which is to say symbol, in the sense of words as well as artifacts—was found to capture his reactions to life, and transmit them.

Culture is by definition individual: the creator acts essentially alone, communing with his own instincts and his own sensibilities. The cultural act is a relationship between an artist's soul (including both the emotional and rational qualities) and the world. Yet the vocabulary is not individually invented—that is logically impossible. The context must be social, interpersonal.[1]

Solipsism, in other words, is refutable easily enough, however deep the truth that no one can ever really know what goes on in someone else's psyche. And language relates to the world wholesale: each word, that is, becomes affected subtly yet irrevocably by every other. No direct one-to-one correlation exists

7

between object and denotation, however much the logical posi-
tivists had hoped otherwise. All language acquisition takes place
in a context.[2] It is no mystery that translations can never be
perfect, for no two languages ever coincide.

This philosophical fact has serious implications for understanding ethnicity: one's native language is a part of one's self.
A person's emotional contact with the sensory stimuli touching
his being are deeply and irrevocably language-specific. Poetry
has been written about this, for even metaphor captures only
approximately so intimate an experience as one's dependence on
language.

One of the most accurate descriptions of how native language
leaves an indelible imprint on the psyche is found in Eva
Hoffman's autobiographical book *Lost in Translation: A Life in
a New Language*. Hoffman is a Polish Jew who recently re-
turned to her native Krakow after having emigrated to Canada as
a teenager in the 1950s. In the following passage, Hoffman
describes her feelings as a newcomer to the Free World, specifically, the dilemma of preparing herself emotionally and psychologically to learn the entire context of another culture's language—understood in its totality, linguistic and extralinguistic.

> [H]ow does one bend toward another culture without falling
> over, how does one strike an elastic balance between rigidity
> and self-effacement? How does one stop reading the exterior
> signs of a foreign tribe and step into the inwardness, the viscera
> of their meanings?[3]

It is not clear that one *can* step into "the viscera" of these mean-
ings, even if one desperately wishes to do so.

Hoffman is astonished by the near-impossibility of translation. She explains how much more there is to it than one-to-one
correlation:

> [T]he translation doesn't work. I don't know how Penny feels
> when she talks about [for example] envy. The word hangs in a

Platonic stratosphere, a vague prototype of all envy, so large, so
all-encompassing that it might crush me. . . .

The result is alienation: in the process of living in a new language, life itself becomes an abstraction, the self is submerged
in a reality it cannot ultimately reach:

[T]his radical disjoining between word and thing is a desiccating
alchemy, draining the world not only of significance but of its
colors, striations, nuances—its very existence. It is the loss of a
living connection.[4]

The all-encompassing aspect of cultural translation indicates
that aesthetic perception is not restricted to linguistic categories
narrowly understood. The same words will refer to very different kinds of objects or attitudes in different cultures—and
their connotations will differ as well. Again Eva Hoffman:

[For me,] English words don't hook on to anything. . . . The
words float in an uncertain space. They come up from a part of
my brain in which labels may be manufactured but which has no
connection to my instincts, quick reactions, knowledge. Even
the simplest adjectives sow confusion in my mind.[5]

Hence a profound sense of disjunction, a loss of identity. For
with language comes an entire galaxy of shared symbols and
behavior-patterns. Their disappearance and denial can be devas-
tating. Writes Hoffman of her feelings in Canada when she first
arrived there:

I have no interior language, and without it, interior images—
those images through which we assimilate the external world,
through which we take it in, love it, make it our own—become
blurred too.[6]

Yet those images make experience as a whole possible. And
experience is indeed holistic, multidimensional. One's feeling

about reality involves conscious and unconscious instruments, not all identifiable by any means. The connection between the verbal and the nonverbal is intricate, ineffable, mysterious. And surely affected by one's ethnic history.

A person approaches the world with considerable background knowledge consisting of a complex set of extra-verbal experiences. Aesthetic experience in particular takes into account this intellectual landscape. It stands to reason, therefore, that geographical setting would affect the colors of one's mental palette, as would the music of a mother's lullaby and the dance and rituals of adolescence. That is to say, in brief, that cultural settings would naturally affect individual perceptions in specific and similar ways.

The idea that a people's aesthetic life is intrinsic to its identity is thus reasonable, indeed commonplace, and has a powerful psychological basis which can in no way be deemed "irrational." On the contrary, it is entirely a part of the life of reason insofar as all language is not only essential to reason but inseparable from it: language is based on logical rules, and makes ratiocination possible.

Yet this is not to say that the concept of ethnic identity in a conscious, politically relevant sense arises somehow naturally. By no means. In the Middle Ages, there generally prevailed at most a visceral, primitive, natural feeling of community of language or homeland. Hard as it may seem to believe in light of recent history, in the eleventh century the word "deutsch" was first employed merely to designate the people speaking the German language, a nationalist tinge having been added no less recently than the seventeenth century.[7]

One of the earliest expressions of nationalism centering on language was found in East-Central Europe: the Hussites waged war against the Germans in 1420 partly to defend "the Czech and Slavonik language." They were in fact successful, capturing many German towns in Bohemia, where the influence of Czech language and literature became important. The socioeconomic consequences were predictable: the educated Czech middle class tried to keep itself in the newly gained official positions by demanding knowledge of Czech as a prerequisite for office.[8]

In the sixteenth century, the golden age of Spain, Castillian became the language of the court and the official language of the country, gaining considerable influence throughout the world—however short-lived, for Spanish culture slowly died out for complex socioeconomic reasons. Across the sea in England, Parliament began holding its sessions in English, and not French, by 1362; English finally became dominant in legal documents by 1450,[9] although French continued to be influential among the educated classes.

It was not until the seventeenth century that modern nationalism was born—in fact, on English soil. One of its first exponents was the poet John Milton (1608-1674), who in his eloquent pamphlet *Areopagitica*, written in 1644, identified nationalism with individual freedom from authority. This liberal twist, happily, continued to color the English brand of nationalism.[10] Imported by France, it took on a rather more collectivist character at the hands of Jean Jacques Rousseau (1712-1778). Hans Kohn summarizes the difference between the English brand of nationalism, which "respected the privacy of the individual: the nation-state was regarded as a protective shell for the free interplay of individual forces," and the French brand, which "stressed that the duty and dignity of the citizen lay in political activity and his fulfillment in complete union with his nation-state."[11]

A final new twist to Western nationalism was added by Rousseau's German disciple, Johann Gottfried von Herder (1744-1803), who first introduced the idea of "folk-spirit" as the principal determinant of nationality. Herder conceived of the community as cultural and spiritual, creating a general will, a *sens commun*. He felt that human civilization is manifested in separate ways through each culture, that men are first and foremost members of their national—and linguistic—communities.

In 1764, for example, Herder wrote that "every language has its definite national character. . . . Perhaps I shall be able to imitate the languages of foreign nations, without, however, penetrating the core of their characters."[12] But Herder was emphatically not a chauvinist. His love for nationality embraced them all: "No love for our nation shall hinder us in recognizing everywhere the good which can be effected progressively only in the great course of times and peoples."[13] It was left to the following century of romanticism to twist these ideas into a virulent—bastardized—form of nationalism.

Scholars have disagreed about the centrality of language to the concept of nationalism. Georg Schmidt-Rohr is one who believes that the community of language is the real national community,[14] while C. A. Macartney argues on the contrary that there are no sufficient objective characteristics—including language—for determining one's nationality.[15] Robert Michels agrees that neither language, nor religion, nor a common past provides such characteristics, but rather "the will of a people," which is "essential."[16] In a spirit of compromise, historian Arnold J. Toynbee says that nationality "can be kindled by the pressure of one or several factors, as a common country, language, or tradition."[17] Historically, it was not until the last century that language became a fact on which the prestige and power of a group depended. Alien languages were used until recently by official bodies, in academic contexts, and among the upper classes.[18]

In the nineteenth century, the idea that a nation's language, territory, and culture forms a metaphysical unity that could be captured by some such concept as "the will of the people" was best articulated by Georg Wilhelm Friedrich Hegel (1770-1831). In his *Philosophy of History*, written at the end of his life, Hegel writes:

> The state, its laws, its arrangements, constitute the rights of its members; its natural features, its mountains, air, and waters, are *their* country, their fatherland, their outward material property;

the history of this state, *their* deeds; what their ancestors have produced, belongs to them and lives in their memory. All is their possession, just as they are possessed by it; for it constitutes their existence, their being. This spirit of a people is a *determinate* and particular spirit . . . [19]

Hegel elegantly, if questionably, passes from the cultural on to a political dimension. For him the state becomes one with its "spirit." Hence various "forms" are identified as belonging to that spirit:

It is thus one individuality which, presented in its essence as God, is honored and enjoyed in religion; which is exhibited as an object of sensuous contemplation in art; and is apprehended as an intellectual conception in philosophy. In virtue of the original identity of their essence, purport, and object, these various forms are inseparably united with the spirit of the state.[20]

Metaphysics aside, there is nothing particularly unusual or untoward about a country taking pride in the accomplishments of its citizens. In addition to the cultural contributions, which include what is traditionally thought of as "the arts"—music, literature, painting, and to some extent philosophy—that touch the emotional side of man's nature, there are also, of course, contributions to science, law, economics, and so on. The great scientific discoveries of a Copernicus or a Marie Curie should be a source of satisfaction to the people of Poland, just as Adam Smith was a credit to his native Scotland. Far from being dangerous, such sentiments are positive and encourage greater creativity as well as respect for others who are equally engaged in advancing knowledge, from which all mankind can profit. Yet clearly, Hegel opened the way to a very different—potentially explosive—unitary conception of national identity, with disastrous political implications. As historian Carlton J. H. Hayes indicates, Hegel's statist nationalism took root in Italy as well as Germany, and was spread by scholars who used his philosophy "for curiously illiberal nationalist ends," culminating in fascism.[21]

Evidently, the idea that a nation possesses a "spirit" involves a metaphysical leap of dangerous proportions. Identifying such a spirit with national identity, moreover, only exacerbates the problem. What kind of entity is this? If it is somehow "unitary," where do minorities fit in—or do they? It is far from clear that tolerance is compatible with this metaphysical model of nationalism.

From the legitimate concept of linguistic similarities and certain cultural continuities that can be collected in some logical fashion and identified with a national or ethnic identity, it does not follow that a monolithic "spirit" emerges as the metaphysical equivalent of a Platonic Idea. Such a reification could only play into the hands of an intolerant nationalist elite—as indeed happened in the form of fascism, a century later. Ultimately, therefore, nationalism became an irrevocably political tool of ruthless groups who used it to further their own interests.

2. Political Aspects of National Integrity

Writes Hans Kohn in his seminal scholarly work *The Idea of Nationalism: A Study in Its Origins and Background*:

> The most important outward factor in the formation of nationalities is a common territory, or rather, the state. Political frontiers tend to establish nationalities. . . . [S]tatehood or nationhood (in the sense of a common citizenship under one territorial government) is a constitutive element in the life of a nationality.[22]

Today, this idea seems commonplace. And indeed people have had strong communitarian feelings as far back as history can be traced. But the political implications of nationalism—the idea that common heritage carries with it special political legitimacy—is very much a modern phenomenon. One of the first to appreciate the significance of state nationalism was the brilliant Niccolo Machiavelli (1469-1527), whose celebrated essay *The Prince* ended with a chapter entitled "An Exhortation to Liberate Italy from the Barbarians."[23] Notwithstanding Machiavelli's reputation as a cynic, it appears that his preference for a strong nationalist state was inspired less by his affection for Italy as a whole than by nostalgia for his native Florence. Hoping that his countrymen would once more become prosperous and virtuous, Machiavelli adopted what looks very much like a pre-Leninist version of belligerent pragmatism devoid of morality. It is not hard to see why he earned a dubious reputation as the first, or certainly one of the first, modern nihilistic thinkers. Writes Machiavelli:

> Where it is an absolute question of the welfare of our country, we must admit of no considerations of justice or injustice, of mercy or cruelty, of praise or ignominy, but putting all else aside must adopt whatever course will save its existence and preserve its liberty.[24]

Machiavelli's approach to nationalism did not take root until three centuries later, with the advent of the French Revolution of 1789. Not that the revolution's intellectual architect, Jean Jacques Rousseau, intended it that way. Rousseau, who is sometimes called "the father of modern nationalism," actually defended the idea of nationalism as a reaction to what he considered the corruption of man's originally good nature by a decadent society and state. Resigned to the fact that man could never again be a "noble savage," Rousseau turned to the state—paradoxically enough, for the state is hardly an instrument that always promotes freedom—to seek redemption. And with this idea, modern democratic nationalism was born. Thus, E. J.

Hobsbawm distinguishes "the revolutionary-democratic" concept of a nation, which developed mainly after the French Revolution, from the concept of "nationalism" proper.[25] To Rousseau's horror had he realized it, the fascist nationalism of the twentieth century was his own version's bastard (yet not unpredictable) heir.

Rousseau's principal aim was to introduce the concept of the sovereign will of individuals uniting in a compact, "the social contract," with one end in mind: the pursuit of happiness by its individual members. And while this contract was ultimately democratic, based on the idea that men were created equal, Rousseau—like his predecessor Montesquieu—was sensitive to the differences that the traditions of history and the conditions of climate and environment, as well as language, produce among different groups.

In Rousseau's last political writings, his *Considerations on the Government of Poland,* as in his *Project on the Constitution of Corsica*, he praised the creation of national character and institutions that are the product of history and education. He encouraged the promotion of games and festivals, opposed the election of foreigners as kings, and demanded universal military service in a national militia, whose first duty was eternal vigilance over the internal liberties of the people. The fusion between the rights of men and their safeguard through the national state was the crucial step in the definition of modern nationalism.

The English were especially keen on safeguarding individual rights within a national state. John Stuart Mill (1806-1873) provided a particularly clear and objective definition of what he called "Nationality" in his essay entitled "Representative Government":

> A portion of mankind may be said to constitute a Nationality if they are united among themselves by common sympathies which do not exist between them and any others—which make them cooperate with each other more willingly than with other

> people, desire to be under the same government, and desire that
> it should be government by themselves or a portion of them-
> selves exclusively.[26]

This indicates that "common sympathies" translate into common
government. Whether that government happens to be democratic
or not appears to be left open. If "a portion" of the group is
chosen—implying either a republican form of democracy or a
nondemocratic arrangement—it still constitutes a "nationalist"
arrangement. But there is little doubt as to where Mill's own
sympathies lay: with a classical-liberal form of government.

It has been generally understood that modern nationalism is
intrinsically a political concept. Mill, however—having witnessed the powerful nationalist currents that swept Europe, and
Eastern Europe in particular, in the Revolution of 1848—believed that ethnic identity must precede national aspirations.[27]
This is not a universally accepted position; for the existence of a
"sentiment" of nationality is difficult to test. It may be impossible to tell whether or not a people or a group possesses the
psychological need to join under "one government." To be sure,
there must be a political intention to do so. Positing a "sentiment" that precedes such an intention could serve as a legitimizing force—but this is philosophically questionable. How
does one know that such a sentiment exists?

Mill writes that the "common sympathies" at the root of
nationalism (or "Nationality") have many causes. Nationalism,
therefore, does not arise from any one cause or any one group of
common traits. Sometimes it is "race and descent"; it may be a
similar language, or religion; and geographical proximity is an
intrinsic factor. The strongest tie, in Mill's opinion, is provided
by political antecedents: a national history and "community of
recollections." This is to say that a kind of collective memory is
invaluable: "collective pride and humiliation, pleasure and re-
gret,"[28] to which Mill might have added, collective hatreds. To
the extent that animosity can be codified through a system of
laws, unfortunately, it becomes explosive.

Some communities, however, are more prepared than others for self-government. Mill recognized this, since it was commonly understood in the eighteenth century—which was, after all, the Age of Reason—that while all men were equally endowed with reason at a certain stage of civilization, that stage, however minimal, did have to be reached. This is not to imply that some communities could not become self-sufficient until their members "matured." Rather, it is to make the point that communities—even within a relatively small geographical area—can develop at very different rates, with serious political implications. Thus, some regions may become urbanized at different rates and experience differences in educational status and religious affiliation, which can lead to political tensions. It is not unreasonable for a group to wrap itself in the honorable mantle of nationalism and "the soul of a nation" to advance its own interests, which may or may not coincide with the interests of the larger political entity.

In purely agrarian societies, the political urgency of appealing to "national" identity seems not to exist. Historically, this phenomenon appears to accompany modern society, coinciding with industrialization and the perception that cultural/historical continuity may be threatened. The threats may be primarily economic, or they may be triggered by foreign occupation and perceived injustices.

To backtrack for a moment: what does it mean to appeal to "nationalism" as a politically unifying concept? The Scientific Revolution of the seventeenth century brought with it a trust in the Law of Reason—to replace, in a sense, trust in the "divine right of kings" that had justified the hereditary monarchy in much of Europe. The concept that the people—limited by the rules of the Law of Reason—are the locus of legitimacy led rather naturally to the idea that "A People," however loosely defined, can constitute a government. More specifically, a particular social class may unite for particular ends to impose its members' will—and institutionalize their interests—under the cloak of nationalism.

While it is ultimately impossible to discuss the connection between "state" and "nation" in completely general and philosophical terms, abstracting from specific historical contexts, attempts have been made. Immanuel Kant (1724-1804), for example, writes in *The Science of Right*, that the state, when viewed in relation to the supposed hereditary unity of a people, constitutes a nation. His skepticism regarding this "hereditary unity" is well captured by the qualifier, "supposed." Kant is evidently unimpressed by the significance of such an element; ultimately, he insists that the state—or nation, so defined—must be subjected to moral laws. The state, after all, is designed to counter the natural propensity of men to wage war against one another—it is not intended as an instrument to wage war more efficiently. And yet the history of East-Central Europe is, above all, proof of just such use of the political tools available through state intervention.

The legacy of the eighteenth century, taken to its logical extreme in the nineteenth century, is by no means limited to exalting the Law of Reason—that is rather the British and American variant. The French took *"liberté, égalité, fraternité"* to romantic heights: Delacroix's picture of the bare-breasted French nation quintessentially captures the erotic, nonrational, inebriating ecstasy of oneness embraced by the figure of "la patrie." Once a political system is perceived as embodying the apocalyptic historical will of the people, danger is imminent.

The ideology that carried this point of view to its logical extreme was Marxism. Even though it was militantly antinationalist, Marxism was based on a conviction that the will of the people—or more specifically, the class will of the proletariat—must be codified in a political system. Marxism—and its logical heir, Leninism—flaunted its hostility to nationalism. Writes Lenin: "Marxism is irreconcilable with nationalism, even the 'justest,' 'purest,' most refined and civilized. Instead of nationalism of every kind, Marxism advances internationalism, the amalgamation of all nations in the higher unity that is growing under our eyes with every verst of railway."[29] Lenin's internationalism culminates in the inevitable march of history toward its own end, the withering away of all class conflict (and hence also, by a relentless logic, all national conflict). Yet nationalism proved to come in handy later in the process of "building socialism." The single-minded, ruthless twist that Lenin added to the dialectic of that system, however, accommodated the change: any number of adjustments and crimes would come to be justified in order to reach the promised nirvana, that blessed dictatorship of the morally pristine proletariat led by a well-organized and truly progressive Communist Party.[30]

But more about Marxism in the next chapter. To return to the political aspects of nationalism, a number of clarifications are in order:

1. Political power may be sought by a national entity to free itself from economic, political, or cultural exploitation by another nation and cultural group.

2. Political power may be claimed by a national subgroup which considers itself to be the true "embodiment" of the national spirit.

3. Political legitimacy may be desired by a culturally homogeneous group whether or not it has a national identity, in order for its members to survive and gain respectability in a political context that it does not necessarily (though it may) wish to replace or fundamentally modify.

Political power may be gained in various ways. A national group may wage war or conduct a revolution and win—thus gaining territory, economic concessions, and some degree of acceptance in the international arena. A group may also demand certain concessions by appealing to bodies that are supposed to recognize "national" claims—such as international organizations that have legitimate standing. Or a long-persecuted group may attempt to set up a nation in a new area, appealing to other countries' sense of responsibility. Generally, territorial attachments are extremely powerful; what dilutes them is ethnic mixtures and a checkered history. In East-Central Europe, with its convoluted series of foreign interventions, there are few pure territorial attachments.

Each of these political issues may be associated with a metaphysical model of ethnicity (as further elaborated in the next section), a model which in turn performs a legitimizing function. It may be noted too that no matter what problems are found with any one of these models, their historical—and psychological—reality cannot be denied. For example, however impossible it may be to prove that a group is the "embodiment" of a national spirit, the facts of both the claim and the belief are politically relevant.

Different nations, obviously, have different political histories. Their experiences with self-government, with enslaving or being enslaved by others, are a part of their national memories. These memories then form part of a nation's "mentality" and its members' attitudes toward themselves and others. They are as important to understanding the complex nature of national self-image as are the linguistic, cultural, and territorial dimensions. In East-Central Europe, the metaphysical models of ethnicity must be understood in relation to the special historical and cultural background of each region. For each metaphysical definition fulfills special needs.[31]

3. Metaphysical Definitions of Ethnicity

The idea of a "spirit" that embodies the nation is the necessary correlate of a politically monolithic concept. There are differences, however, in how man's relation to the universe within a national context has been explained. While some philosophers have looked more to the psychological dimension, others have conceived of nationalism as a designating term—whether it encompassed a nation as a whole or some quintessential part (say, the peasant, the king, the church, the poet, etc.).

Many twentieth-century scholars have claimed that nationalism is nothing more than "a state of mind."[32] One may sketch some of the definitions.[33] For example, John Oakesmith calls nationalism "what the vast majority of civilized people feel to be the most sacred and dominating inspiration in life"—with emphasis on the "feeling."[34] Friedrich Otto Hertz distinguishes "national consciousness" from "legal nationality," "cultural nationality," and "political nationality." The latter, he feels, depends on national consciousness, which he feels "cannot be observed and measured by exact methods."[35] In a more empiricist vein, Florian Znaniecki defines nationality broadly as "a collectivity of people with certain common and distinctive characteristics."[36] Similarly, Karl W. Deutsch defined a people in terms of its system of social communication.[37] It was only after the French Revolution that the people (in fact, the third estate) became identified with the nation; generally, the concept of the nation had included only the upper stratum of society, as opposed to the common folk.[38]

What may be called "group consciousness" or a state of mind arising from a certain sensitization, however, appears to be a necessary component of nationalism. This requires a certain degree of social awareness or "consciousness," to use a Marxist or at least idealist term—thereby recognizing that it is not "natural" or inborn. Positing such an awareness would not imply the existence of a "thing"—unlike "spirit," which implies some sort of real entity, however ethereal.

Aristotle (384-322 B.C.), for example, felt that love of family, home, and community was natural—but not beyond a very small community. Voltaire (1694-1778) also noted that the larger "la patrie," the weaker the feeling of identification with it.[39]

On a different metaphysical level, nationality could be identified with the relationship that a people feels with God and the universe: the Jewish nation, for example, considers itself to have had a special relationship with Jehovah, and Christians feel an eschatological tie to the Messiah. Hans Kohn explains that "three essential traits of modern nationalism originated with the Hebrews: the idea of the chosen people, the emphasis on a common stock of memory of the past and of hopes for the future, and finally national messianism."[40] Yet the history of Europe until the end of the Middle Ages stressed mainly the general and the universal rather than the parochial and individual, or the national and idiosyncratic.

Primitive societies had an intimate relationship with nature, on a cyclical basis—as evidenced in the rituals centering around the seasons, the harvest, and other natural events including birth, puberty, and death. To label these feelings as "nationalism" proper would be highly misleading. But they too represent an important component in the family of psychological phenomena involved in the concept.

The quintessentially modern metaphysical definition of nationalism as the "spirit" of the people presupposes cultural homogeneity, which is in turn embodied in a common political tradition. This Hegelian reification of a psychological phenomenon is similar to a religious concept: positing a reality beyond any individual, which consists of an entity that is much harder to determine, verify, and defend. The Platonic conception of a state/nation as an organism predated the Hegelian "spirit" and was probably the first rationalist embodiment of this concept. Yet its degeneration into a romantic and idealist entity is easy enough to anticipate.

Whatever form "the nation" may take, the relevant point is the existence of a need to define it somehow, if only in psychological terms. In other words, it does not seem to have sufficed to make reference to such facts as the propensity to favor one's immediate family, or neighbors, or even kinsmen. In some fashion, "nationalism" seems to have required an existence beyond the empirical facts about human nature. But positing such a metaphysical entity has generated intractable problems.

The ensuing proliferation of posited "spirits of the nation" proved remarkably pernicious, capable of justifying lethal impulses. It may be that the supposed existence of entities like a "national spirit" made it easier to exploit and even kill in their name.

The metaphysical "nation" is most problematic when defined in racial terms. The idea of a "race" is notoriously shaky. No sufficient genetic or cultural traits can define this concept, particularly as applied in Nazi (and pre-Nazi) Germany. The Austrian writer Robert Musil (1880-1939), writing in his 1921 essay " 'Nation' as Ideal and as Reality," described with contempt the entire pseudoscientific literature on race:

> This literature is concerned not with measuring skulls, eye color, or skeletal proportions, which interest only a few, but with qualities like religious sense, integrity, state-building power, scientific ability, intuition, a talent for art, or tolerance of ideas: things of which we hardly know how to say anything at all about what constitutes them. This literature ascribes or denies these things to supposed "races" with the help of an anthropological pig-Latin because it can instill dignity in the nation through its ear by ventriloquizing with the voice of the ages. One cannot deny that a good part of our national idealism consists in this diseased way of thinking.[41]

In brief, then, an important—perhaps principal—function of the metaphysical description of any one definition of nationalism is to construct a justificatory mechanism for certain kinds of actions. These actions may range from promoting certain cultural forms at the expense of others to discriminating against—even murdering—other human beings. Metaphysics, in other words, precedes and sometimes promotes genocide.

4. Aggression and Struggle for Power
Disguised as Nationalism

One of the most popular ways of defining nationalism is in terms of a struggle for power: as a cynical tool to achieve power, pure and simple. The earliest anti-nationalist warning was delivered by Lord Acton in his 1862 essay "Nationality":

> Nationality does not aim at either liberty or prosperity, both of which it sacrifices to the imperative necessity of making the nation the mould and measure of the State. Its course will be marked with material as well as moral ruin, in order that a new invention may prevail over the works of God and the interests of mankind.[42]

Similarly skeptical, Elie Kedourie, who had great respect for Lord Acton, writes that "nationalism is a doctrine invented in Europe at the beginning of the nineteenth century. It pretends to supply a criterion for the determination of the unit of population proper to enjoy a government exclusively its own."[43] Specifically in Eastern Europe around 1800, where there was no industrial middle class, little by way of an intelligentsia, no national governments, and virtually no industrialization—with the exception of a few areas in Bohemia and Silesia—a number of people were dissatisfied with their lot. "These people imported nationalism to Eastern Europe," writes Peter Sugar,[44] implying a conscious and deliberate, even if not necessarily sinister, enterprise.

Even a cursory look at the history of the Balkans in the past millennium indicates that the degree of human misery, the exploitation, and the cynical use of state organs to take advantage of the weak, murder one's various enemies, and elbow one's way into the world, could not have failed to leave deep traces of animosity, even undying hatred. And while on many occasions the ethnic identity of the oppressed could be considered a motivating factor, generally it seems that a large array of cultural, educational, and other socioeconomic factors were at least as significant. Surely the intelligentsia of Eastern Europe (of the Serbians, Czechs, Slovaks, Jews, Ukrainians, Poles, Romanians, etc.) imported the concept from France, England, and Germany, adapting it to their special historical and economic circumstances.

To turn briefly to the economic aspects of nationalism, mercantilism (the belief that a nation's industry had to be regulated by government to "protect it" against competition from abroad) was surely a crude attempt to institute the idea that individual well-being could be secured only by the economic power of the nation. The Industrial Revolution, moreover, seemed not to dampen nationalist feelings of protectionism.[45] Known also as "economic nationalism" (as well as "neo-mercantilism," to underscore its subsequent evolution), the idea is based on the theory—not usually grounded in fact—that people of one nation must be protected against the inroads of other people.[46]

There are, of course, many more-recent echoes of this concept. In the context of East-Central Europe, with small countries finding themselves being traded, ping-pong style, among powerful super-neighbors such as France, Austria, and Russia, it is not difficult to empathize with attempts to gain some sort of relief. The ability of American revolutionaries to gain independence from what they saw as unfair taxation without representation by the king of England must have filled the people of East-Central Europe with awe. Alas, they did not have the geographical advantages of the Americans, who were an ocean away from the Crown.

Nationalism, of course, may be invoked in the name of escaping aggression or may be used to justify its infliction upon others. There are political reasons for appealing to nationalism that differ from context to context. Unless these motivations are understood, faced squarely, and dealt with appropriately, nationalism will not be properly appreciated, but either unnecessarily glorified or vilified. To say this, however, is not to imply that once a motive is unmasked, once the dubious ulterior purpose is revealed, all problems are solved. Aggression is no less real and no less dangerous for being called by its true name. The task does not stop at analyzing group psychology.

But it does start there. Robert Musil, for example, graphically described the intoxicating, indeed erotic, feeling that had engulfed the nations of Europe before World War I. It could not be denied, wrote Musil, that mankind "was touched at that time by something irrational and foolish, but awesome," with enormous potential for evil. Its essence lay in the obliteration of the individual:

> One suddenly became a tiny particle humbly dissolved in a supra-personal event and, enclosed by the nation, sensed the nation in an absolutely physical way. It was as if mystical primal qualities that had slept through the centuries imprisoned in a word had suddenly awakened to become as real as factories.[47]

And suddenly millions of people, "for the sake of the nation, ran into the arms of death." Calling it "a monstrous hysteria," as Musil does, will not eliminate it—anymore than would the use of this expression even more appropriately in the context of the Second World War deny the very real feelings that motivated the Holocaust.

The feelings of anxiety, of hatred, of the need for self-importance gained at the expense of destroying others, have always been in need of antidote. One of the most effective such antidotes, originally, was religion wedded to an enlightened concept of the people or the nation. Specifically, the Jewish tradition held that God had made a covenant with the people of Israel so as to insure the respect of His commandments. These commandments, however, applied to all people and were meant to bring happiness and justice. Christianity, in a similar manner, was intended to apply to all men; notwithstanding the close relationship between the Church and particular political bodies—that were later to become nations—the Judeo-Christian legacy has been essentially universalist in nature.

Anthony D. Smith denies that religion ever provided the basis for nationalist identification. While religion—for example, Orthodoxy in Romania—may have preserved a sense of community, especially after the Middle Ages, Smith says: "between traditional religion and nationalism there is a decisive break." At most, "religion often provides the sociological material for nationalism to work on, but it does not and cannot explain the latter's character or appearance."[48]

Yet particular religious leaders have often been less than faithful to the principles they espoused. Through the ages, individual members of the Church have been corrupt and manipulative, often using the pulpit to further their own ends, as have different social groups and individuals seeking power and influence. A cynical enough look at history indicates that nationalism became a fig leaf for human aggression almost from the outset—and even religious communities were not immune.

The potentially dangerous aspects of nationalism were captured by Carlton J. H. Hayes, writing in 1926, in the following list of evils:

> An intolerant attitude and behavior towards one's fellows; a belief in the imperial mission of one's own nationality at the expense of others, particularly at the expense of backward peoples; a habit of carrying a chip on one's national shoulder and defying another nationality to knock it off; a fond dwelling on the memory of past wars and a feverish preparing for future wars, to the neglect of present civil problems; a willingness to be led and guided by self-styled patriots; a diffidence, almost a panic, about thinking and acting differently from one's fellows; a spirit of exclusiveness and narrowness which feeds on gross ignorance of others and on inordinate pride in one's self and one's nationality . . . [49]

—to mention but the most important.

The recognition of a deeply opportunistic and myopic quality to nationalism is particularly useful in assessing an essential aspect of the post-Communist phenomenon that is too ambiguously identified as "nationalism" *tout court*. There are many complex elements involved in the transition from Communism to democracy, and nationalism is only one of the factors that can easily mask other hostilities and fears. Thus, the civil war that ravaged Yugoslavia in 1991 played out some of these hostilities, with nationalism as the wild card beneath which much was hidden. The vicious events in that country, it is fair to say, surpassed most people's expectations, their virulence both frightening and unrelenting.

In brief, nationalism can become not merely a vehicle for self-advancement but a veil for the most murderous impulses of human nature. Thus, the sophistic garb that would pave the way to the Holocaust began with the idealist precursors of German racist nationalism in the nineteenth century, notably Friedrich List (1789-1846) and later—his anti-Semitism undisguised—Heinrich von Treitschke (1834-1896). As K. R. Minogue explains, what started out as a revolt against external rules, a yearning for spontaneity, a repudiation of the mob, became the supreme mob-rule: "the time was to come when Hitler would be able to turn virtually the whole German population into a herd by the simple expedient of explaining to them that, racially speaking, they were all essentially leaders."[50]

Thus the herd became evil incarnate—the banality of evil stunning in its vulgarity, terror, and ubiquity. Sigmund Freud (1856-1939) had no illusions about man's propensity to do evil under various euphemistic guises. He reasoned that deep-seated aggressive tendencies ultimately of sexual, libidinal origin—were channeled in the context of society to lead to mass-movements of incalculable power. What nationalism does, above all, is construct an entity—the nation—which may or may not be easily identifiable with a political state. That entity is superimposed upon its individual members, to provide those members with a superstructure that becomes a source of moral approval unthinkable in its absence. The so-called "good of the nation" can then be used to justify the most heinous of crimes.

Writing in "Thoughts for the Times on War and Death," Freud notes that nations, which "are in a measure represented by the states which they have found," act in far more reprehensible ways than do particular individuals. A state at war, for example, "permits itself every such misdeed, every such act of violence, as would disgrace the individual man."[51] Mob psychology transforms the worst instincts and magnifies them.

Freud does not pretend to be able to explain this phenomenon. Rather than dignify it with clinical labels, he expresses dismay at the irrationality of violence:

> Actually why the national units should disdain, detest, abhor one another, and that even when they are at peace, is indeed a mystery. I cannot tell why it is. It is just as though when it becomes a question of a number of people, not to say millions, all individual moral acquirements were obliterated, and only the most primitive, the oldest, the crudest mental attitudes were left. Possibly only future states in development will be able in any way to alter this state of affairs.[52]

Freud is suggesting, in other words, that the aggressive chauvinistic, xenophobic, and racist brand of nationalism is a primitive stage of development—a precivilized stage. In that, he is correct. It is important to remember, however, that "primitive" does not mean "prehistoric." It can happen again even today, as the presumably sophisticated twentieth century draws to a close. This has been, after all, the most bloody century in history. One can only hope that the next millennium will be an improvement, but there are no guarantees.

II

The East-Central European Context:
Post-Communist Trauma

1. The Marxist-Socialist Legacy

While it was explicitly anti-nationalistic, Marxism paradoxically served some of the same functions as nationalism: it provided a sense of group identity beyond the individual; a messianic sense of history; and a moral framework designed to justify aggressive acts against others, who were perceived as exploitative, in a power-struggle for social, political, and cultural control. The appeal of Marxism can be explained at least in part in terms of these dynamics. Slovak writer Martin Simecka elaborates: "Nationalism is similar to communism in some ways. It gives people an ideology, a sense of identity that we lost when we became free."[1] In short, people need a way to identify themselves—a common fate to transcend individual loneliness amid the insecurities of the free market and before the finality of death.

Four decades after its forced imposition in East-Central Europe, Marxism has left deep, possibly even inescapable scars. Continues Simecka: "People are used to thinking in ideological terms. Nationalism, like communism, gives people a sense of being for or against."[2] In brief, nationalism is the new euphemism—the mantle that covers a multitude of both sins and vir-

31

tues—with the resulting confusion that is the necessary correlate of all ambiguity. Despite their different histories, therefore, the nations of East-Central Europe are now facing a number of common problems that can be traced to their recent ideological plight. These problems are the reason why today more than ever the Danubian nations constitute, in the words of Hugh Seton-Watson, "the sick heart" of modern Europe.[3]

Undoing a distorted view of history

Over the past four decades, each nation of East-Central Europe has had to systematically rewrite its entire chronology from a Marxist-Leninist point of view. Regardless of the relative value of each nation, the valor of its people or its cowardice, the richness of its culture or its mediocrity, erasing the nation's history altogether might have been easier to survive than the distortion. Books must now be rewritten, rediscovered, resuscitated.[4]

By way of example, after the Communist takeover in Romania, the Romanian Academy's linguistic work—especially the dictionary of seventeenth- and eighteenth-century Romanian—was designed to prove that Romanian was really a Slavic language rather than a modern version of the Latin imposed by the Romans in the first century A.D.[5] Distortions of history of this sort by Communist rulers play into the hands of the post-Communist manipulators, the demagogues attempting to instill an idyllic nationalism.

Coping with a sense of wounded pride and lack of self-esteem

Having had to lie—not only about one's own past, but even about the present, about matters before one's own eyes—for fear of the secret police, for fear of destruction and retaliation not only against oneself but one's own children and parents, has created a deep sense of insecurity. No matter how clear it is that such fear is perfectly justified, the sense that one should have sacrificed everything in the interest of truth is impossible to erase completely.

Vaclav Havel described the essence of this process, in his now-famous essay "The Power of the Powerless," as drawing

> everyone into its sphere of power, not so they may realize them-
> selves as human beings, but so they may surrender their human
> identity in favour of the identity of the system, that is, so they
> may become agents of the system's general automatism and
> servants of its self-determined goals, so they may participate in
> the common responsibility for it, so they may be pulled into and
> ensnared by it, like Faust with Mephistopheles.[6]

This Faustian legacy weighs heavily on the people of East-Central Europe. Havel's—and Aleksandr Solzhenitsyn's—chosen method of salvation, "living in truth," cannot help those who, sometimes quite deliberately, usually half-consciously, and sometimes even unconsciously, went along with the Big Lies of their corrupt Marxist regimes. They cannot forgive themselves.

An additional source of self-loathing is the absence of genuine culture during the Communist period. For in addition to the virtual obliteration—certainly distortion—of past tradition, there was the *klisch* of socialist anti-art, the mirror of the lie in the form of pseudo-culture that needs to be undone, to be eliminated from the body of the nation like so much poison, without the benefit of antidote.

Facing the effects of economic trauma

The legacy of poverty that the people of East-Central Europe are having to face is not only a source of anger as a result of the felt injustice at having been subjected to a system imposed by force. It has also manifested itself in the form of exhaustion because of malnutrition, unspeakable pollution, psychological stress, and lack of proper medical attention and treatment. What is more, the contrast with life in the West makes it harder to bear: penury in the Middle Ages was taken as a given; in the twentieth century it is the insult added to the ideological injury. Fortunately, and somewhat surprisingly, there is a greater degree of resilience than might have been anticipated.[7]

Disintegration of genuine fellow-feeling

Paradoxically, one of the saddest legacies of the supposedly anti-individualist Marxist-Leninist dogma, which turned out to be an enormous hoax benefiting a small ruling elite, is the pervasive suspicion of one's fellow human beings. In a social setting where The Group was exalted beyond all individuals—requiring immediate reporting of any deviant behavior that was supposed to harm Group Interests—suspicion became inevitable. It is impossible to properly appreciate the true nature of post-Communist nationalism without understanding this fact.[8]

Alongside suspicion of one's own countrymen there has also been deep mistrust of foreigners—though different nations have been viewed differently, of course. The West in particular has been mistrusted for the rather palpable reason that it did not come to the rescue of East-Central European nations during the time of Soviet occupation. On the contrary, various forms of détente with the Communist rulers were witnessed by the people with incredulity. The entire system finally collapsed of its own weight in 1989, no thanks to Western accommodationism.

Hatred came easily in an atmosphere that has been called (to use Josef Zverina's expression) "a whole ideology of hate":

> This ideology justified everything it required; everything was permitted to achieve its success; it encouraged hatred and even

required it on occasions. There can be no worse threat than this
to human morality and life. While, unhappily, we find hate in
various guises all over the world, hate here has its specific features. The education of a people into a single permitted ideology
creates a much more intensive basis for such hatred. Hate is
thereby "nationalized," as it were.[9]

The legacy of hatred could not but express itself in pathological forms of human interaction after the fall of Communism.

Reinventing language

Marxist Leninist "newspeak" was designed specifically to affect people's perceptions of reality, to make easier the distortions
that had been required by socialist reconstruction. New words
were invented, old ones redefined. Slogans permeated ordinary
speech, and some words became outlawed outright. People's re-
lationships with each other were redrawn in the attempt to create
"the new socialist man." In the process, one became alienated
from one's most immediate instrument of communication with
one's innermost reality: language. Never before had such an
experiment been undertaken. For the imposition of a foreign
dialect or an alien tongue does not affect one's original language.
This was rather a mutilation, a sacrilege—and was perceived as
such.

Coping with post-Marxist secularization

The physical destruction of churches, the co-opting of the
clergy (in many cases recruiting its members to serve the secret
police), the declaration of atheism as the official philosophy
(while denouncing religion as so much "cultism"), and the closing of schools of theology—all this served in many cases to kin-
dle interest in religion rather than muting it.[10]

Yet it would be wrong to underestimate the importance of an atheistic philosophy on the population at large. It may be a long time before the people of East-Central Europe gain a healthy perception of their metaphysical place. Twentieth-century Western secularism has caught them unaware, leaving them in the midst of the universe God-less, helpless, equipped mainly with their conviction that unless they help themselves probably no one will.

Facing maneuverings by the outgoing nomenklatura

In addition to the traumatic legacy of Marxism-Leninism, there remain the maneuverings of the outgoing *nomenklatura*, the privileged elite of the socialist state. This class did not disappear with the revolutions. The old elite is undoubtedly seeking all possible ways to survive. In each of the countries of East-Central Europe, the former Communist ruling class has found ways to capitalize on the dismantling of the empire. In the process, the predictable fueling of discord, the creation of instability and discontent, including anti-Semitism, will continue to take place. And it will not always be easy to detect the causal elements.

As Michael Dobbs observes, "for thousands of mid-level Communist *apparatchiks*, nationalism has represented an almost miraculous way of hanging on to power following the collapse of Marxist-Leninist ideology. By handing in their party cards and wrapping themselves in the national flag, former Communists were able to acquire new political identities overnight."[11] There seem to be similar motivations—and similar tactics—in the peculiar hard-line nationalist/Stalinist approaches of Albania, China, North Korea, and Romania. Vladimir Tismaneanu believes that the Communist leaders of these hapless countries shared a "magic-ritualistic conception of the omnipotent and omniscient Supreme Leader,"[12] subjecting their people to an uncommonly ruthless oppression, often poorly understood in the West.

Perhaps the most spectacular—and sinister—example of a change of ideological facade may be found in former Serbian President Slobodan Milosevic. Says Dragan Veselinov, a political scientist at the University of Belgrade:

> Milosevic and the Serbian Communist elite were not originally nationalists. They took over nationalist ideology to keep themselves in power without substantially changing the political and economic system. By switching ideologies, they were able to unify the public mind, achieving the same result as under Communism.[13]

This is not to say that the *nomenklatura* cannot be enlisted in the democratization process—indeed, elements of the old regime will undoubtedly contribute to building the new. The problems arise when they attempt to use non- or even anti-democratic methods to protect their privileges. Generally, power tends to corrupt even former opposition leaders once they are in control. This has been the case, for example, both in Georgia and in Moldova, where duly elected leaders turned out to have less respect for democracy than might have been expected, once they were exposed to the sweet aroma of authority. Need one even mention that the attraction to power is not a monopoly of Marxists?

It is no exaggeration that in East-Central Europe, the insidious, skillful, and astute efforts on the part of the old elite to change their stripes is perhaps the most formidable obstacle to the dismantling of the old regime in the near term. In Bulgaria, for example, Turkish party spokesman Yunal Lyutfi puts it plainly: "Nationalism is the only card the Socialists [the former Communists] have to play. Regrettably, that feeling is flourishing in this part of the world. It has no future, but in the short term it is very dangerous."[14] And it is not clear how short the "short term" may be.

Zlatko Anguelov, Bulgarian editor of the London-based *East-European Reporter*, also observes that a climate of "hysteria and hostility" surrounding the issue of nationalism and the Turkish minority is being manufactured:

> The blame for this unhealthy environment must be laid at the door of the Communists, as in a number of other East European countries where they have attempted to prolong their grip on power by stirring up essentially a pseudo-question.[15]

This "pseudo-question" he believes to be the issue of "pseudo-nationalism." But "pseudo" does not mean "bogus." It is a very real problem indeed, which has already poisoned the body and soul of Bulgaria's newborn democracy—not irrevocably perhaps, but deeply, and for a long time to come.

2. The Historic Legacy of Nationalism in East-Central Europe

It is possible to talk about a special brand of nationalism in Eastern or East-Central Europe, explicable by a complex variety of factors shared by the ethnic communities in the region, however different the particular circumstances at any particular time. Walter Kolarz refers to the people of the region as "peoples without history" in one specific sense, borrowing the terminology of Friedrich Engels, on the ground that in feudal times only the upper classes wielded effective political power, while the people themselves "were condemned to be inarticulate, anonymous, silent."[16] The result has been an uneven development in the self-awareness of these ethnic societies, the ordinary folk alternately revered and despised, their languages either ridiculed or glorified, depending on ideological and political expediency. By contrast to Western Europe, where relative national homogeneity had been achieved before the nineteenth century,

East-Central Europe continued to accentuate and nurture differences. Royal power helped unify and civilize the West more rapidly, while in the East "feudal and local particularism did not yield to political and administrative centralization until the nineteenth century, when nationalism was becoming a conscious force."[17] Accordingly, rather than naturally tending toward democracy, the East tended toward exclusiveness, particularism, and intolerance. Isaiah Berlin speculates—perhaps a bit unfairly—that the reasons may be found in historical impotence:

> Those who cannot boast of great political, military or economic achievements, or a magnificent tradition of art or thought, seek comfort and strength in the notion of the free and creative life of the spirit within them.[18]

Put bluntly, East-Central European development, both political and economic, lagged behind the West. Hans Kohn explains that in this region

> nationalism arose not only later, but also generally at a more backward stage of social and political development: the frontiers of an existing state and of a rising nationality rarely coincided; nationalism, there, grew in protest against and in conflict with the existing state pattern—not primarily to transform it into a people's state, but to redraw the political boundaries in conformity with ethnographic demands.[19]

These demands were in many ways understandable. Over the centuries, the people of the region were variously occupied by the Turks under the Ottoman Empire, the German Empire, the Austrian Hapsburg monarchy, and the Russian Empire. When nationalism was discovered—mainly by the nobility in the occupied lands of East-Central Europe—the process was tinged with pathological, even irrational elements. Thus, Kohn contrasts it, somewhat simplistically but not unjustly, with Western nationalism, which was at least originally "based on reality," while "nationalists in Central and Eastern Europe created, often out of myths of the past and the dreams of the future, an ideal fatherland, closely linked with the past, devoid of any immediate connection with the present, and expected to become sometime a political reality."[20] Kohn is perhaps unduly charitable to Western nationalists, who after all had their share of intolerance. But in the East the problem was unquestionably worse. The nationalism based on dreams and myth was particularly undemocratic and illiberal.

On occasion, it was outright messianic, especially when special privileges were claimed for an entire people, as was the case in Poland and, at later stages, in Hungary. But as Peter F. Sugar observes, "messianism cannot be egalitarian; it claims rights for a chosen people, the *Volk*, not for the individual or citizen. This *Volk* concept is practically totalitarian."[21] The reason seems clear enough: the *Volk* idea stands for a group, with a history and national traits expressed through culture and community. The individual is nothing outside of his group. If he opposes the majority he is a traitor to his whole tradition, to his kind.

The *Volk* approach to nationalism in East-Central Europe was radically different from the romantic concept developed in the West, in particular the idea developed by Johann Gottfried von Herder at the end of the eighteenth century. Herder's emphasis was on linguistic and cultural tradition; he was fully aware of the dangers behind an overly messianic rediscovery and rewriting of national history. Presciently anticipating later abuses, he warned that "the historian of humanity should be careful in this [the rediscovery of the past] not to make one nationality into his exclusive favorite"; nor should anyone be tempted to force his own nationality's system upon others by virtue of national prerogative, no matter how well-intentioned the motives, for "the happiness of one nationality cannot be forced upon, thrust upon, or loaded on another or all others."[22]

Herder's humanistic tolerance did not survive the adoption of his ideas in Eastern Europe. Though he is credited with having been extremely influential in introducing nationalism in Eastern Europe—Germany being the main transmitter of ideas to that region—Herder became distorted almost beyond recognition. While he was a champion of liberty for all humanity, his disciples to the east were statists and exclusivists.

He would hardly have anticipated that one of his most widely acclaimed contributions to the East-Central European nationalist awakening was to be the praise he reserved for the Slavs, whom he admired particularly for their humble devotion to peace and their refusal to compete for the mastery of the world, patiently paying their taxes in exchange for tranquility. Herder's one fatal mistake was to add that several nations, but mainly the Germans, "committed crimes against them"[23]—thus fueling the most virulent form of Pan-Slavism, especially among the Czechs and Slovaks.

The Slovak Lutheran minister and poet Jan Kollar (1793-1852), for example, who acknowledged his debt to Herder, chose to thoroughly distort Herder's admiration of the Slavs, turning it into a caricature as he predicted that "everywhere the Slavs, like a mighty flood, will extend their limits" as "sciences will flow through Slav channels; our people's dress, their manners and their songs will be fashionable on the Seine and on the Elbe."[24] So much for the mild-mannered Slavs.

It is notable that the champions of this aggressive nationalism were the intelligentsia—poets, writers, members of the educated class. Until the beginning of the eighteenth century, they had used French, German, and Latin as their languages. But in the 1780s the Hapsburg monarchy unwittingly sowed the first seeds of its own demise. Emperor Joseph II not only introduced religious tolerance but encouraged education, which at the lowest level was to be given in the vernacular language, thus creating new cultural elites among the people of East-Central Europe. In addition, Herder's philosophical support for folk traditions and native language further encouraged these elites "to write grammars and compile dictionaries of their native tongues, to translate

foreign works, to collect folk songs, to explore national antiq-
uities, to do research in historical chronicles and archives."[25] All
this was meant to enhance the glory of one's nation and establish
not its equality among others but indeed its superiority morally,
historically, and even religiously.

In some cases, the first stirrings of nationalism came through
religious awakening and the sharpening of religious conflicts.
This was the case, for example, in Poland, where Catholics and
Greek Orthodox citizens clashed during the late eighteenth century. After Poland was first partitioned in 1772 between Prussia,
Russia, and Austria, Jan Dekert, then mayor of Warsaw, organized a movement for the civil and political rights of burghers.
The following year, Polish was introduced as the language of
instruction in the universities. Bishop Adam Naruszewicz wrote
a history of Poland, and more foreign books were translated into
Polish, while old Polish texts were being edited and reprinted.

The second partition of Poland in 1793 was followed by
another in 1795, the sad result of a Polish revolt against the
Russians led by Tadeusz Kosciuszko. Kosciuszko had been a
veteran of the American War of Independence, which evidently
inspired him to emulate the exercise in his native land, but with
far less propitious results. It was not, however, until after the
great uprising of 1848, when the nationalities of East-Central
Europe revolted against the Hapsburg monarchy demanding
greater self-determination, that Polish—and East-Central European—nationalism came into its own.

In Poland, its eloquent spokesman was Adam Mickiewicz, a
professor of literature in France at the time of the 1848 uprising,
whose nostalgic attachment to his native land was romantic and
benign. His *Books of the Polish Nation and of a Polish Pil-
grimage*, written in 1832, is a beloved classic, having helped
keep alive the national consciousness of his people.

Another veteran of 1848 who left an indelible mark on the
history of nationalism in his country was the Hungarian lawyer
Lajos Kossuth (1802-1894), who galvanized an already aggres-

sive political nationalism. Writes Kohn: "Whereas the nationalist activities of Czechs and Croats, Romanians and Ukrainians, were before 1848 mostly confined to the cultural field, the Magyars in Hungary turned to transform this ancient multi-racial kingdom into a Magyar national state."[26] This is not to say that nationalism in Hungary did not start in a similar cultural context. George Bessenyei (1747-1811), an officer at the court of Vienna, was instrumental in having books translated from French and English into Hungarian. Debreczin, the largest Hungarian city, then became a kind of national center. A new Hungarian newspaper, *Magyar Hirmondo*, recommended wearing national costumes, and the old Hungarian leaders who had resisted Tatars and Turks were being revived and revered. The first history of Hungary was written by Stephen Katona in 1778, and another, forty-volume version occupied him from 1779 to 1817.

In 1833, the official language of Hungary was changed from Latin to Magyar, thus starting the process of Magyarization of the Hungarian administration. Lajos Kossuth edited the progressive newspaper *Pesti Hirlap*, which demanded constitutional reforms, liberal legislation, and national independence for Hungary—an admittedly enlightened position, but with one catch: these rights were not applicable to the non-Magyar minorities.

Indeed, the spirit of 1848 soon turned sour as nationalist aspirations undermined the democratic ideals that inspired the uprising in the beginning. The new nationalism stressed collective power and unity at the expense of individual freedom. East-Central European nationalism took a turn against liberalism with a vengeance.

Hungary seemed to win out, however, at least relative to other nationalities. In 1867, Emperor Francis Joseph of Austria was obliged to share power with Hungary, inaugurating the so-called period of Dualism known as Austria-Hungary. Afterward, Hungary was regarded as a "national state" with one "political nation"—the Magyars. (The word for "Magyar," for example, is in fact the same as for "Hungarian.") Membership in this nation had been limited in past centuries to the nobility; in 1848, as a result of the liberalizing trend, it extended to all those who spoke Magyar and considered themselves Magyars.

But it went no further. While members of other nationalities (*nemzetiseg*) could continue using their own languages in private, the public language had to be Magyar. In 1868, a Nationality Law was passed that allegedly protected the cultural rights of the non-Magyars, but in effect many of their privately financed schools were suppressed; education laws introduced more rigid regulations about the teaching of Magyar, and non-Magyar newspapers were either undermined or suppressed outright, which produced bitter anti-Magyar nationalist activity.

Shortly after the dramatic awakening of the Hungarians, others followed suit. Nationalist demands were raised by Romanians, Serbs, Slovaks, and Croatians who lived on the territory of Hapsburg Austria—all wanting educational reforms, the right to learn in their own languages. Their limited success relative to the Hungarians was due to their smaller numbers, their more dispersed settlement patterns, and the fact that their nobilities were weaker.[27]

The region was indisputably transformed by the upheavals of 1848, which were widely perceived to be nothing short of a "watershed." Sugar describes the ensuing period succinctly:

> [B]etween 1848 and 1914 nationalists faced two enemies: the dynastic empires from which they wanted to obtain at least autonomous self-rule and all the other people who shared their goals but also claimed some of the same territories, and the same determination to be recognized as sovereign over them. What emerged was something like a *quod licet Jovi non licet bovi* [what is permissible for Jove is not permissible for the bull] attitude of denying others the rights, privileges, and even the validity of dreams perfectly justified for one's own nation.[28]

This exclusionary attitude created the xenophobia, anti-Semitism, and other noxious fumes that persisted through the First

World War and were only exacerbated by the horror that ensued with the Nazi period and the Communist totalitarian terror. The attitude is emerging now in a newer form, having been distorted during the Communist era when cynicism of a Marxist-Leninist variety gave the concept a peculiar twist: paying lip-service to ethnicity within an ideological context that had nothing but contempt for it. This situation presents new dangers in a volatile region facing not only insuperable economic problems but also deep psychological scars—some of them perhaps beyond repair.

Not unexpectedly, ethnicity figured rather prominently in the rise of Communism in the region. Writes Richard V. Burks, in his study *The Dynamics of Communism in Eastern Europe*:

> We may erect almost as a principle the proposition that in [E]ast-ern Europe numerically weak ethnic groups produce above-average numbers of Communists, providing these groups have a traditional or ethnic tie to Russia. Other factors being equal, the weaker the ethnic group, the greater the proclivity.[29]

In other words, members of groups that were less integrated turned in greater numbers to Communism as a source of power. The conclusion seems inescapable that Communism was seen as providing a certain political advantage, leaving the impression that for many opportunism played a role in the selection of this ideology.

Once Communism came to power, the new governments used nationalism in various ways, "using and exploiting it when it suited their convenience, while condemning it in theory."[30] For instance, the Soviets called on the Czechs and Poles to unite behind the Soviet Union against the Germans. Similarly, Russian nationalism itself—previously condemned by Stalin as high treason—became a useful tool in his hands during the Second World War.

During the Communist regime, moreover, nationalism was used as a "cover" for what were actually economic demands and grievances. One reason was that it safer for people to express their grievances in such terms—since economic reforms as such were virtually beyond hope in rigid, centrally controlled socialist systems. This pattern cannot be ignored if one hopes to understand post-totalitarian East-Central Europe.

III

Spotlight on Romania

1. The Pre-Communist Tradition

To summarize very briefly Romania's historical odyssey, the Carpathian-Danubian area was originally populated by the Dacians (or Getae) in the first half of the first millennium B.C. until their conquest by Rome in the beginning of the second century A.D. The Latin language and Christianity were gradually introduced over the course of the next century. But the Romans were forced to leave Dacia in 261 A.D. by nomadic tribes—opening the region to waves of such invasions. In the eleventh century, Transylvania (Dacia's northwestern region) came under Hungarian rule, which lasted until 1918. Wallachia and Moldova (the southern and eastern regions, respectively) were briefly united by Michael the Brave from 1593 until 1601. After his assassination, there followed Turkish influence in the provinces, mainly through Greek officials known as Phanariotes (after the Phanar quarter of Constantinople where the Greeks originated). The provinces had to pay tribute to the Turkish sultan for over two centuries.

During the 1700s, Russia and Austria vied with each other for Romanian territories. Russia briefly occupied Moldova, then

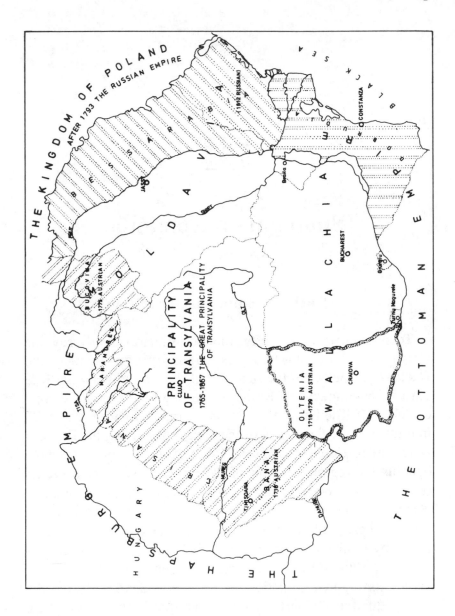

Wallachia, Moldavia (Moldova), and Transylvania, end of the
eighteenth and beginning of the nineteenth centuries.

Austria took parts of Bukovina (a small region north of Moldova), followed by Russian occupation of Bessarabia (to the east of Moldova). In 1859, Wallachia and Moldova were united under Prince Alexandru Ioan Cuza, who was simultaneously elected by both provinces. King Carol succeeded Cuza in 1866 and finally expelled the Turks in 1877. Having joined the Allies in the First World War, Romania (which included Moldova and Wallachia) was rewarded its largest territory ever in 1920, including Transylvania as well as Bessarabia and Bukovina. Romania lost the latter two provinces to the USSR in 1940 at Stalin's diktat, which Hitler endorsed. Northern Transylvania was briefly lost to Hungary that same year but regained after the war. Present-day Romania, then, is not as large as it could be—lacking notably the provinces annexed by the Soviets—but it certainly includes most of the traditionally Romanian land.

Romanian nationalism dates from the eighteenth century, particularly in Transylvania. Its linguistic idiosyncrasy—a Latin island in the Balkans—helped to distinguish the nation from the Hungarian, Slavic, and German ethnic groups surrounding it. As Stephen Fischer-Galati points out, "the thrill of tracing the spoken language of the Romanians of Transylvania to the inhabitants of ancient Rome arrested whatever thoughts of social and political justice they might have entertained."[1] Translated in political terms, this discovery, or rather rediscovery, of a distinguished cultural/linguistic heritage led to the petition known as *Supplex Libellus Valachorum* sent to Emperor Leopold, whereby the Romanians asked the Hapsburg ruler to grant them the same rights as those enjoyed by others in the province of Transylvania. More specifically, "them" meant the elite—the Romanian bourgeoisie, higher clergy, and intellectuals, definitely not the peasants.

The late historian Vlad Georgescu also believed that the awakening of Romanian ethnic consciousness was the result of discovering the existence of common roots and tradition despite constant exogenous political divisions:

Ethnic consciousness, the Romanians' first step toward national
consciousness, arose from the discovery of their origins and
their unity of language and culture, and the realization that they
were divided into three separate states [Wallachia, Moldova, and
Transylvania] for purely political reasons.[2]

Yet the vehicle that crystallized ethnic consciousness was
seventeenth-century historiography, culminating in the work of
Dimitrie Cantemir (Prince of Moldova in 1693 and again in
1710-1711), who documented the common origins of the Romanians and their continued presence in the territories. Georgescu
credits Cantemir's prestige with the fact that his writings helped
ethnic consciousness spread among political leaders and intellectuals, "and became the theoretical basis of the national consciousness of a few generations later."[3] This is not to say that
Cantemir intended to promote political unification and activism;
that was to come.

A contemporary of Cantemir who was visibly influenced by
his writings, Bishop Ion Inochentie Micu-Clain (1692-1768),
was also instrumental in arousing Romanian self-consciousness,
but from a religious perspective. In the absence of a national
aristocracy, it is not surprising that the clergy should have taken
on the task of seeking Romanian political rights. After his
appointment in 1729, Clain embarked on a campaign to raise the
social and political standing of the Uniate (Romanian Catholic)
clergy, hoping as well to raise the Romanians of Transylvania to
a level of equality with other nations in the area. He used the
word "nation" in a number of different ways, on occasion referring to members of the Uniate Catholic church but at other
times referring to the sense of a community held together by
common origins, customs, and religion. There is no doubt that
he wanted to ease the burden of the Romanian people and in
particular that of the peasants, arguing that the "Romanian nation" was more numerous and contributed more to the state than
any of the other nations in Transylvania.

Clain's conception fell short of later nationalist theories because the common people were not quite considered full members of the nation. What is more, ethnic unity did not extend to Romanians living across the Carpathians.[4] It fell to the next generation of Uniate intellectuals to develop an elaborate ideology of Romanian nationhood based on the doctrine of Daco-Roman continuity.

This generation—which included Petru Aron, Grigore Maior, and Silvestru Caliani—attempted to define the concept of the Romanian nation in a grand and ambitious manner; they made efforts to reconcile a number of disparate concepts—specifically, the rural and Orthodox tradition with the intellectual modernity of the West. The term "Romano-Valachus," used by the people of the region to describe themselves, emphasized the Latin tradition of Romania, but had no traces of chauvinism or hostilities.

It is interesting, in fact, that in Romania such emphasis was being placed upon rediscovering the nation's past, when some modern thinkers in the West at that time regarded the past as backward and inferior. But for Romania a metaphysics of nationality still had to be created to justify a new sense of pride and self-assertion.

The contribution of religious figures to this awakening should not be underestimated. Bishop Ioan Lemeni of the Romanian Uniate Church and Bishop Vasile Moga of the Romanian Orthodox Church joined forces in 1834, asking the Hapsburg rulers to grant the Romanians full constitutional rights equal to those possessed by their Magyar, Szekler, and Saxon neighbors in Transylvania. In 1837, Moga petitioned to obtain relief from taxes and tithes for his clergy, and on several subsequent occasions both Moga and Lemeni sought greater religious freedom. These efforts, however, were unsuccessful, and gradually the influence of the church in Romanian life, and the bishops' influence in particular, began to be challenged in the 1830s and 40s. A number of prominent intellectuals—notably Samuel Clain, Gheorghe Sincai, Petru Maior, and Ioan Budai-Deleanu

—advocated the use of reason as a way of promoting Romanian nationalism. Through them, the Enlightenment reached the easternmost shores of the Danube.[5]

One of the most significant Romanian representatives of the Enlightenment was Simion Barnutiu, a philosophy teacher at the Uniate lyceum in Blaj in the early nineteenth century. A Kantian, he recognized the moral equality of all men and extended the concept of human rights to groups or nations, since he believed that people develop in groups, rather than as atomized individuals.[6] In fact, he described the struggle for self-determination in terms of the natural order of things—this was a thoroughly secular initiative.

And indeed some serious frictions developed between the intellectuals and the religious sector. The feeling of the intellectuals was that church government had gradually but unmistakably become too aristocratic and rather unresponsive to the needs of Romanians as a whole. The struggle between these two social and political segments of Romanian society was to continue with various ebbs for subsequent decades, its remnants never entirely eradicated.

This is not to say that many Romanian intellectuals were not deeply religious. For example, the enlightened vicar of the Orthodox Church in the late nineteenth century, Andrei Saguna, who believed that nations had to be guided by the eternal moral values, felt that the rituals and practices of the Romanian Orthodox Church were peculiar expressions of the Romanian soul. Yet at the same time he believed in a strict separation of church and state, and opposed the clergy's participation in political affairs.

Yet neither he nor the intellectuals were able to prevent the passage in 1868 of the so-called Law of Nationalities, which had been designed to provide for some legal protections and guarantees for the Romanians under Magyar rule in Transylvania, but which in fact failed to do so. The Romanians regarded this law as a disaster—the intellectuals and the religious community trading blame among themselves. The subsequent history of Romanian nationalism continued to be characterized by strife between the intellectuals, who gained greater control over the political life of the country, and the church hierarchy, whose power was weaker yet whose influence—through the educational system—rendered it the most significant force in preserving Romanian nationality.

It appears that Romanian nationalism as developed in Transylvania was actually less elitist and more enlightened than the brand found in the other two main Romanian regions—Wallachia and Moldova. Gradually, Moldova became more democratic and assumed a Francophile form based on constitutionalism and natural rights. In 1821, Tudor Vladimirescu led an unsuccessful but bloody revolution, forging a bond between the nationalist leadership of Wallachia and the peasant masses. Independence, both cultural and political, from Greek Phanariotes, Slavic Russia, and the Ottoman Empire, became a rallying cry of both Moldova and Wallachia.

It was the revolution of 1848 which swept throughout Europe that finally mobilized and consolidated Romanian nationalism. Social reform then became an integral part of the philosophy. Two particularly strong intellectual exponents of liberal nationalism who gained considerable political significance in the late nineteenth century were C. A. Rosetti and Ion C. Bratianu. Rosetti, a poet and political activist, believed in a united Romania on the ground that "the people of Wallachia and Moldova are members of the same nation, both of them bear the glorious name 'Romanian,' they speak the same language, they belong to the same church, their interests are identical, they had to suffer through the same things, and they have the same ideas about what they should do to make things better for themselves."[7] And from an economic point of view, Rosetti believed that unification would reduce government spending—a quintessentially liberal perspective. Indeed, Rosetti—who in 1843 had organized, with two other Wallachian liberals, Nicolae Balcescu and Ion Ghica, a secret society called *Fratia*—passionately believed that all men were created equal, a conviction shared by Bratianu.

Yet Bratianu, leader of the Liberal Party and later prime minister, felt compelled to slightly reconstitute Romanian history in order to support his nationalist and liberal beliefs.[8] He argued that the Romanian tradition of freedom dates to the nation's origin in the first millennium, claiming that the Romanian people had inherited this tradition from republican Rome. This explains "the miracle that a nation of ten million could preserve the traditions of democracy faithfully and clearly. It is a nation of ten million people which is more Roman than the Romans themselves and which is ready, even to this day, to embrace new ideas of justice and brotherhood."[9] In a hyperbole that is perhaps understandable, Bratianu felt that the mission of Romania was to set an example for the region—to be "the only representative of democracy in Eastern Europe."[10]

The difference between these two liberal thinkers is that for Rosetti the question of a free society always preceded the nationalist question, while for Bratianu nation and freedom were interlinked.[11] Yet theoretical niceties aside, Rosetti and Bratianu both provided an important footing for Romanian nationalism of the following (twentieth) century. Andras Keszthelyi summarizes their contribution as follows:

> Rosetti kept struggling to apply the terms of Western European political thinking to a society different from those of Western Europe. He was struggling to convince the majority, which was indifferent concerning a revolution, of the necessity of political emancipation. Bratianu, by contrast, had to rewrite history for lack of suitable traditions.[12]

The legacy of rewriting history was to plague Romania thereafter. Keszthelyi notes that it was Bratianu who thus decisively influenced the course of political rationalization in that country—with aggressive nationalism increasingly dominating and winning over the liberal nationalism Bratianu had originally defended.

The question of historical accuracy is, in fact, at the heart of the Hungarian-Romanian conflict which has always plagued Transylvania, especially in the last two centuries. According to a new report by the Commission on Security and Cooperation in Europe, *Minority Rights: Problems, Parameters, and Patterns in the CSCE Context*, "academic conferences have been convened to debate the question of who settled in Transylvania first, or who has maintained the longest continuous presence in the region. . . . According to the Hungarian version, the Romanians did not appear in Transylvania until the 13th century, when nomadic shepherds migrated in from Wallachia,"[13] while Romanians themselves trace their ancestry to the Dacians. The belief that continuous presence was the basis for claiming territorial rights was not, of course, universally held. Foremost among the exceptions was the historian and philosopher A. D. Xenopol, who wrote in the last decade of the nineteenth century—in his seminal *History of the Romanians of Trajan's Dacia* (1889-93)—that the main basis for territorial claims lies in the right to self-determination.

There are, to be sure, other important reasons for divisions among these two major ethnic groups: most Hungarians—and Germans are either Catholic or Protestant, while Romanians are generally Orthodox. Transylvania, moreover, was under Hungarian domination until 1918. Hungarian efforts to Magyarize the region, whose majority population was Romanian, inevitably left deep scars.[14] The abuses of the Hungarians, however, were fully compensated in ruthlessness under the dictatorship of Nicolae Ceausescu—to which we shall turn in the next section.

But Romanian nationalism cannot be fully understood without an objective comparative analysis of the national forces—including economic, political, and religious ones—that governed in the area throughout modern times, involving both the Austro-

Hungarian empire and the Russian empire to the east. The result is a complex mosaic of perceived and real wrongs, and attempts to gain justice.

While the details are countless, one conclusion emerges: the beginnings of nationalism in Romania were neither virulent nor xenophobic. Yet the positive elements—a sense of cultural pride and an appreciation for economic fair play—were later displaced by other far more toxic elements. And at all times there was a sense of siege—a sense of wounded pride, a sense that the Romanian nation had been exploited.

The idea of unification of all three main Romanian principalities (Transylvania, Wallachia, and Moldova) became a reality once more—after its brief implementation during the last decade of the sixteenth century by Michael the Brave—only in 1802, through the works of Wallachian Naum Ramniceanu, and then in 1804, by the Transylvanian Ioan Budai-Deleanu. In 1852, Dumitru Bratianu gave the concept life by coining the term "Greater Romania." The political reality of unification dates from 1881, when the Romanian National Party of Transylvania united Romanians on a common political platform in order to fight what they considered to be a process of Magyarization and to regain Transylvania's autonomy. In 1882, the associations Carpati and Astra were formed to help Romanians in their struggle for liberalization. In 1891, the Cultural League was established in Bucharest, changing its name in 1914 to "The League for the Political Unity of All Romanians"—finally showing its true political colors.[15]

Alongside the exclusivist nationalist movements, however, there were also—both on the Hungarian and the Romanian side—artistic, literary, and political movements whose principal aim was the peaceful and cooperative approach of mutual respect and toleration.[16] Writes Vlad Georgescu: "The dominant idea in nineteenth century Romania, nationalism, had appeared before 1800 with a desire for political and cultural regeneration and was

consummated early in the twentieth century when the three principalities united as Greater Romania."[17]

Ethnic conflicts between Hungarians and Romanians were
inseparable from other political and ideological issues. For
example, (Hungarian) Prince Bethlen of Transylvania instigated
the Romanian royal army's intervention in suppressing the
Communist Hungarian regime in 1919—a clear case of class
solidarity over national/ethnic sympathies.[18] But mistrust between these two ethnic groups has obviously characterized their
relations at least for the past century.

No more so, however, than has mistrust of Jews in Romania,
partly for historic economic reasons. During the nineteenth
century, it became the practice for boyars, the Romanian upper
class, to lease their large estates to Jewish middlemen for a fixed
rent, which meant that the Jews were the ones to deal directly
with the peasants and bear the brunt of their discontent. The
great peasant uprising of 1907 was thus directed primarily
against the Jews, many of whom were brutally slaughtered.[19]
Even after 1866, when Jews were allowed to become Romanian
citizens, hardly any were naturalized. Since it was illegal for
Jews to own agricultural land, they were driven to the towns,
but they were excluded from professional careers, public service, and chambers of commerce. While the constitution of 1923
established universal suffrage, anti-Semitism was hardly eradicated from Romania.

The rise of fascism joined the more virulent Hungarians and
Romanians at least in anti-Semitism—there being both a Hungarian and a Romanian variety, the Arrow Cross and the Iron
Guard, respectively. While the Iron Guard, formed in 1927
under the name "the Legion of the Archangel Michael" (its
better-known name dates from 1930), was certainly anti-Semitic, anti-Western, and messianic, this movement was at least
initially rather more religious and nativist in nature, and more
concerned with establishing the Romanians' place in history than

with murder.[20] The movement's ties to the Nazis and the Italian fascists came later. Outlawed first in 1931 and then again in 1933, the Iron Guard reappeared in 1935 under the blatantly nationalist name "All for the Country."

Difficult as this may be to believe, the intellectuals behind the Iron Guard movement were often highly learned, and eager above all to place their nation on the European map. Virgil Nemoianu, for example, cites as one of the factors contributing to this movement the perception on the part of an aspiring national middle class that the social slot of the bourgeoisie was already occupied by ethnically alien populations, including Hungarians, Saxons, and Jews; another factor was the prestigious role model—as well as funds—provided by political elites in Germany and Italy.[21]

Foremost among the intellectual founders of the Iron Guard movement was Nae Ionescu, a professor at the University of Bucharest, who authored a radical program envisaging a political, cultural, and spiritual regeneration for Romania. Its proponents saw themselves as saviors of Romania's soul—which inevitably soon became inextricably linked with a scurrilous, and entirely gratuitous, anti-Semitism.

Nae Ionescu and journalist and poet Nichifor Crainic were leaders of an intellectual circle preoccupied with the relationship between traditionalism and modernism, the concept of the Romanian national character, and the role of Orthodox religion in Romanian society. Ionescu (no relation to the famous playwright Ionesco, his contemporary, who was rather anarchist-liberal in outlook) considered Orthodoxy as quintessential to the concept of Romanian-ness.

To be sure, the Romanian fascist movement was ideologically complex and was seen by many members of the political and cultural elites of Romania in the 1930s as left-wing, or Bolshevik.[22] Anti-Semitism was a natural—indeed Marxist— ingredient of the movement, since the fascists regarded the

Jewish bourgeoisie as a fifth column of the imperialist world-system and an alien, corrupting influence. (This view was consistent with Marx's analysis in his notoriously anti-Semitic and anti-capitalist essay "On the Jewish Question.") Other intellectuals of the Romanian right, however, avoided the more extreme expressions of nationalism. Lucian Blaga, for example, attempted to find a philosophical approach to the Romanian spirit through the Romanian landscape, and the Dacian heritage.

The spiritual-mystical framework of Romanian fascism initially gave it a patina of respectability, but was soon replaced by sheer terrorism. Indeed, the legionary movement brought a perversely quasi-religious death cult to Romanian politics. Mythic qualities were attributed to the sinister fascist leader Horia Sima ("He has the form of an angel and the sword of an archangel. . . . Horia is thought, Horia is feeling, Horia is our light, our will, and our strong arm"). Echoes of the later, no less monstrous, cult of Ceausescu are here already clearly discernible.

The crushing defeat of Romania's military fascist regime by Russian Communism was viewed by many as "the nadir of Romanian nationalism," according to Stephen Fischer-Galati.[23] (To be sure, the mystical nationalism of the Iron Guard had already collapsed in 1941 at the hands of General Ion Antonescu, whose national ideology was rather more traditionally militaristic and conservative.) Yet the newly introduced internationalist ideology of Marxism-Leninism was slowly abandoned in favor of a nationalism whose main purpose was to secure mass acceptance of a highly unpopular revolution. The virulence of that revolution would soon become apparent.

For while it was by no means able to obliterate the philosophically superior tradition of a nonbelligerent Romanian nationalism, Romanian fascism left a deep imprint on Romanian self-conception. The disingenuous nationalism of Romania's post-World War II Communist leadership—which distorted Romania's own history and culture in special ways to fit the new ideology—was accompanied, especially during the Ceausescu years, by chauvinism, anti-Semitism, and xenophobia.

2. Communism with a Nationalist Face

Nicolae Ceausescu, who ascended to power in 1965 as a result of Machiavellian maneuverings extraordinary even by Romanian standards, did not invent the concept of "Communism with a nationalist face." Aside from the Yugoslav model—and its various twins in East-Central Europe, which blossomed on occasion by way of resistance to the Soviet cultural, political, and economic totalitarian straitjacket—there was a Romanian variety cultivated by that country's first Communist president, Gheorghe Gheorghiu-Dej. Dej had resisted Soviet efforts to turn his country into a Communist breadbasket, opting instead for the more traditionally Marxist industrialization approach—which economically was far more deleterious to Romania. In addition, Dej attempted to find some kind of legitimacy for his infinitesimal Communist Party—and to deflect Nikita Khrushchev's suggestions that it was time to de-Stalinize—by eliminating Jews and Hungarians from the top leadership.[24] The Romanian leader thus also tried to offer a national(ist) alternative of sorts by exploiting long-repressed xenophobic sentiments among the pro-Communist "intelligentsia." Yet writer and dissident Dorin Tudoran finds that this "move did not make the Party into a more patriotic organization." On the contrary, "it merely created the [later] nauseating spirit of national Communism."[25]

Vladimir Tismaneanu calls the Romanian variety of national Communism "National Stalinism," and regards it as "a symptom of degeneration."[26] Without wishing to appear to endorse other varieties of national Communism, Tismaneanu nevertheless notes their relatively benign nature by comparison, often reflecting a spirit of reform from within. Not in Romania; the spirit of crass nationalism was anti-reform in virtually every way.

That spirit was perfected by President Nicolae Ceausescu, who shared with Dej a total lack of commitment to the good of his nation, and a megalomaniacal desire to resist even the mighty Soviets in the interest of boosting his own power and place in history. The result was a veritable caricature of nationalism constructed out of a monumental castle of lies and sycophantic anti-history, coupled with one of the most ruthlessly terrorist systems of modern times.

Ceausescu's address to the Constituent Assembly in August 1965, deliberately designed to inspire national pride, illustrates the point:

> Unlimited opportunities loom on the horizon; no previous generation has been fortunate enough to participate in such grandiose social changes, to be on the threshold of national glory. What greater wish could anyone have than to take part in the struggle and work for the attainment of his country's glorious future, for the progress and prosperity of his Fatherland?

In reality, what Ceausescu had in store for his country was a standard of living that earned the former breadbasket of Europe the nickname "Ceaushima"—so named after the Japanese city destroyed more quickly but with comparable horror. The whole world was soon to learn this, by discovering the infamous orphanages that an ABC documentary film has rightly called "The Shame of a Nation."

To fool his people, Ceausescu recreated the past with a vengeance. The obsession with a risibly deformed "history" was in fact his movement's principal similarity to its predecessor, the Iron Guard. Writes Vlad Georgescu:

> It fostered a neonationalism strongly reminiscent in some respects of the one practiced by the Romanian right in the 1930s: emphasis on Dacian, as opposed to Roman, ethnic roots;

constant appeals to historical symbols and myths and affective
identification with figures from the national past as devices to
legitimate present policies; hyperbolic claims regarding Romanian historical and cultural achievements, promoting an inflated
national ego; and indirect encouragement of xenophobic, pseu-
dopatriotic attitudes, including anti-Semitic, anti-Russian, and
anti-Hungarian ones.[27]

Yet Ceausescu's true colors did not become visible to
Western leaders and opinion-makers until the late 1980s. Even
Romanians were fooled at first. Ceausescu's misleading defense
of the liberalizing efforts in Czechoslovakia during the Prague
Spring of 1968 was a brilliant disinformation device. Vladimir
Tismaneanu explains: "Unfortunately, many Romanians were
convinced that Ceausescu was honestly interested in national
autonomy. They gradually discovered that patriotism was only a
technique of social control and personal dictatorship."[28] It is this
legacy of cynicism that has left its strongest imprint on the post-
Ceausist—though hardly post-Communist—system in place in
Romania today.[29]

It also made it difficult to be a dissident in Romania during the
1970s. When the writer Paul Goma challenged Ceausescu in the
early 70s, he was immediately stigmatized as "playing into the
Kremlin's hands." Any opposition was seen as undermining the
national "monolith." Razvan Theodorescu, a former university
professor and art historian whose sympathies turned somewhat
pro-National Salvation Front soon after his appointment as
chairman of Romanian television in 1990, has said that Ceausescu's unquestionable popularity after 1968 is easy to explain:
"Imagine a state of affairs where all the traditional values, all
great literature, music, and art, whether Shakespeare, Gains-
borough, or Handel, were banned or made subordinate to an
alien culture and ideology. That was the situation of Romania
until the early sixties."[30] However exaggerated (and indeed inaccurate) this view of Ceausescu as a champion of cultural
renaissance, there was certainly much hope that the new leader

would be more liberal and more enlightened than his predecessor. This euphoric support of Ceausescu proved premature—the worst was to come soon. In the early 70s, the "cultural committees" of the Culture Ministry established publication priorities, in effect institutionalizing self-censorship. The writer Gabriela Adamesteanu observes that this self-censorship was a very well-entrenched phenomenon indeed.

By the early 1980s, all typewriters had to be registered to the police—a highly effective deterrent to unofficial publishing of any kind. Next came the lying on a monumental scale, about everything from food statistics to infant mortality. The sudden power cuts that led to baby-incubator shutdowns, the incessant cold, hunger, and terror—enforced by an extremely efficient Securitate[31]—that defined life in Romania in the last decade were serious contributing factors in a general atmosphere of subhuman existence.

The Hungarian minority inevitably fared even worse; its cultural and linguistic identity were under serious threat, especially after 1956, the year of the anti-Soviet uprising in Hungary, when Gheorghiu-Dej realized with dismay the strong impact of those events on Hungarians in Transylvania. The "Romanization" of the Communist Party was coupled with the closing of Hungarian schools, so that by the mid-1960s there were unofficial reports that separate Hungarian-language schools no longer existed.[32] The famous Bolyai University in Cluj (Kolozhvar) was forcibly merged with the Romanian Babes University. Nicolae Ceausescu, then Politburo member and Central Committee secretary in charge of cadres, reportedly presided at the meeting where this merger was decided. The university's Hungarian rector committed suicide to protest this coercive policy aimed at destroying the Hungarian minority's cultural identity.

During the Ceausescu years, especially by the mid-1980s, the plight of Hungarians deteriorated—as was spectacularly demonstrated by the move to recycle Hungarian Bibles sent from the

West into toilet paper. History textbooks concentrated exclusively on the Romanian contribution to Transylvania. In December 1984, television broadcasts in Hungarian were terminated, as was virtually all radio programming. And the "systematization" program implemented most vigorously after 1988—a plan to raze about half of Romania's nearly thirteen thousand villages—was the most drastic attempt to completely destroy Hungarian culture.[33] The Hungarian community thus produced a virtually automatic dissident community which opposed these brutal policies.[34]

The tradition of Romanian dissent was also present, but understandably limited under the unusually harsh circumstances of Ceausescu's rule. A notable exception was the "Noica school," so called after the late Constantin Noica, a spiritualist/existentialist philosopher who died in 1987, whose efforts could be summarized as an attempt to find a European path to Romanian self-identity. Katherine Verdery finds that "Noicans (notably Gabriel Liiceanu [currently editor at the Humanitas publishing house] and Andrei Plesu [who became Minister of Culture after January 1990]) presented an image of philosophy and of Romanian culture that was European above all, that tied Romanian identity to 'universal' European values."[35] More than the master himself, Noicans saw the great tradition of Western culture as providing a necessary and natural background for the development of Romanian philosophy.

Another Romanian philosopher who maintained an independent point of view is Mihai Sora, who became Minister of Education after January 1990. Sora's philosophical writings, while cryptic (for obvious political reasons) and seemingly quite esoteric, offer—by his own account—metaphysical grounding for political pluralism.[36] (It came as no surprise, for example, that Sora defended in January 1990 the separation of Romanian and Hungarian schools in Transylvania in the interest of fostering cultural integrity.)[37]

By way of contrasting ideology, a group that Verdery identifies as the "ethnophilosophers" emphasized the unwritten accumulation of popular (rather than learned) philosophical wisdom—a wisdom that Romanians acquired somehow by osmosis. This was an essentially anti-intellectual, primitively populist view, which its proponents found in such official—yet thoroughly nonintellectual—locations as the Institute of Philosophy and the Stefan Gheorghiu Party Academy.

The anti-Western line may be illustrated as follows:

> The archaic form of Romanian philosophy is to be identified with *unwritten philosophy*. It is an *implicit philosophy*, unsystematic, a state of the spirit, a spiritual attitude, a protophilosophy.[38]

This attitude is identified as "Dacian," and considered "a perennial value"—by contrast with Western imports. It is interesting that these "ethnophilosophers," their Communist ties notwithstanding, were even antithetical to Marx: after all, he too was a Western philosopher. Verdery, however unsympathetic to the "ethnophilosophers," finds that both they and the Noicans provided an alternative to the official Marxist point of view, in that they each offered proposals for a "true" Romanian identity and a "genuine" Romanian culture. She notes that this discussion meanwhile "was producing a fundamental construct that was never called into question: the notion of 'the people' or 'the nation' for whom values were being debated."[39] Nationalism was being introduced as a first principle, an unquestioned and unquestionable premise. This much seems clear.

While it may be debated whether the "ethnophilosophers" were truly presenting a dissenting point view or rather a different kind of Ceausist approach to nationalism, the fact remains that an alternative to the ruling Marxist dogma seems unthinkable today without some reference to "the people" and "the nation." Post-Communist nationalism is, in other words, not an option but a necessity. This sad reality is one of the principal reasons why neo-Communism continues to be a real, indeed formidable, danger—for it has learned how to manipulate language, by inventing euphemisms, in the service of statist political ends. And nationalism is an emotionally charged concept whose susceptibility to manipulation is legendary.

3. Post-Ceausist Manipulations

The legacy of anti-intellectualism is the deliberately populist theme embraced by the amorphous National Salvation Front (NSF) in the May 1990 elections—a theme which gave it an overwhelming victory. Those elections, if not "free" in any reasonable Western sense of the word, certainly were not rigged, and are widely accepted as having reflected popular sentiment at the time. It is significant certainly that the Front portrayed the candidates of the main opposition parties as "willing to sell out" Romania to foreign capital, as intellectuals who were out of touch with ordinary people. "While we were suffering under Ceausescu, they had coffee and croissants in Paris" was one popular slogan. President Iliescu's widest popularity was in the country and among blue-collar workers.

Without question the most alarming and aggressive anti-intellectual outburst in East-Central Europe was the miners' brutal suppression of students and intellectuals in Bucharest in mid-June 1990, which had all the marks of a pogrom. An astonishing 67 percent of those polled by the Romanian Institute for Public Opinion Research supported the government's appeal to the miners and 55 percent approved of their arrival.[40] Classical scholar Andrei Cornea, writing in 22, the journal of the independent Group for Social Dialogue, finds that the image of the Jew as the rootless cosmopolitan individualist, supported by and supporting foreign capital, has been supplanted by an identical image of the intellectual.[41]

It was not surprising, therefore, that the NSF would make common cause with the extreme-nationalist, anti-Hungarian organization Vatra Romaneasca (Romanian Hearth), which was established in January 1990 to oppose Hungarian demands for equal rights and ethnic recognition. Several prominent sympathizers of VR were co-opted by the NSF and elected on its lists in May 1990. The first issue of the NSF daily *Azi* (Today) included an article by a member of the VR—playwright Ion Coja—whose references to Hungarians were plainly racist. Nor does *Azi* restrict itself to Hungarians (and, need one add, Jews); it has recently started a venomous campaign against Romania's Uniate community as well.

In addition, a weekly journal, *Romania Mare* (Great[42] Romania), was started under the editorship of Corneliu Vadim Tudor and Eugen Barbu, both former Ceausescu sycophants with notorious ties to the Securitate. This journal is rumored to be receiving funds from an émigré who amassed a fortune in Italy and is purported to be a former sympathizer of the Iron Guard.[43]

The fact that former Ceausescu sympathizers are involved in what is a clearly anti-democratic, hate-mongering group should come as no surprise. They—and indeed the group in power, the NSF—are exhibiting the same lack of concern for the people that was cultivated to an art by their former boss. Writes Nestor Ratesh:

> An arsenal of rumors, manipulation, demagoguery, class and ethnic hatred, xenophobia, and fear was unleashed by the insecure front [NSF] with little regard for the moral and political health of a society that emerged ailing and dehumanized from more than four decades of totalitarianism.[44]

Perhaps we should not be surprised at the NSF's extraordinary success in deceiving and manipulating internal Romanian sentiments—a task which is, after all, facilitated by the still-extensive censorship over Romanian television and by the widespread fears of the tired, tortured population. But what is truly alarming is the disinformation that is reaching even Western public opinion.

The anti-Semitism which has spread like wildfire throughout the country in the aftermath of the revolution has led, for example, Rabbi Moses Rosen to urge the emigration of all eighteen thousand Jews left in the country. Since most of these are old and since they hardly constitute a significant force in Romania, one must wonder about the logic of such a campaign. It turns out that the tactic is not entirely unreasonable.

In the first place, the fact that former Prime Minister Petre Roman is Jewish allowed it to look as if he were a target of anti-Semitic rhetoric, thus in principle turning him into an object of sympathy—and distancing the government from the xenophobic elements in the society. What is more, the government could, in principle, argue that it alone stood between order and fascist chaos. There are a few problems, however, with these hypotheses. For one thing, Mr. Roman published his baptismal certificate and did not appear to have the strongest sympathies for the Jewish community. What is more, when Minister of Culture Andrei Plesu, a former dissident, refused to give *Great Romania* permission to publish, Roman personally reversed that decision. And in February 1991, in an interview with the Hungarian-language television, Roman stated that he was not a member of the Romania Mare foundation, but added that he failed to see what would be wrong if he eventually became a member.[45]

Encouraged by its success, *Great Romania* became a political party (GRP) in May 1991. Its president is Tudor, with Barbu as first vice president. Another vice president is Mircea Musat, who for many years was in charge of distorting Romanian history as an "instructor" with the Ideological Department of the Romanian Communist Party's Central Committee, promoting the extreme nationalist line. Reminiscent of its fascist predecessor, the GRP appeals to the image of the blood-soaked ancestral soil. Michael Shafir elaborates:

For Tudor and his friends the supreme value is the nation,
which is perceived as being under a historically uninterrupted
siege, having to fight against both foreign and internal machina-
tions aimed at bringing about its dismemberment. . . . The two
main components of the GRP ideology, as reflected in the
party's main documents and in the discourse of its leadership,
are a past-oriented appeal to traditionalist communitarian (as
opposed to individualist) values; and an implicit (rather than
explicit) drive to bring about a more "balanced," and hence more
positive, reconsideration of the "achievements" of the communist regime.[46]

And while the NSF government has recently come under
criticism by this new neo-fascist party, the original relationship
was certainly cozy: as late as June 14, 1991, the Minister of the
Interior awarded a prize to the editors of *Great Romania* for
"high-level professionalism" and "patriotism." In an interview
that same month, Romanian Information Service spokesman
Nicolae Ulieru openly came out in defense of this publication
and praised it for its popularity with the readers. This collaboration between former Ceausescu cronies and the post-
revolutionary government has been one of the more sinister
developments in East-Central Europe.

There is little doubt that the journal *Romania Mare* and the
organization Vatra Romaneasca have enjoyed the support of
former Securitate members. VR's statement of principles con-
tains the strongest endorsement of the Securitate. And it is
notable that Ceausescu himself is lauded by the same statement
as a good Romanian patriot. Meanwhile, VR's principal target is
the Hungarian community—alongside the Romanian democratic
intellectuals. In this campaign, VR has had the full support of
the NSF, which sometimes portrays opposition leaders as in fact
Hungarian (thus human-rights activist Doina Cornea, for example, was identified as Doina Juhasz—her Romanian husband's
Hungarianized name—while National Peasant Party leader Ion

Ratiu was amazingly referred to as Racz Janos.)[47] This leaves the Hungarian opposition with few alternatives but to adopt a defensive and highly charged attitude.

4. Uneasy Options for the Opposition

The minorities in Romania today must live with the fact that an organization such as Vatra Romaneasca states in its "Secret Program Statement" of February 20, 1990 (which the organization repudiates), the following strategy:

> The popularity of Vatra Romaneasca will be secured throughout the world by way of propaganda activities, appealing to the anti-Hungarian, anti-Gypsy and anti-German sentiments which have deep roots in the souls of Rumanians. From the very outset, we want every Rumanian to be clear about our final goal: a Greater Rumania in which alien elements have no place and will not be tolerated.

This kind of attitude leaves little room for subtlety.

What appalls Hungarians today, moreover, is that VR continues to be influential. And the acts of the Romanian government—occasional protests to the contrary—play right into the hands of VR supporters. Hungarians continue to hope for the restoration of Hungarian-language television broadcasts of serious length, permission for Hungarian students to study in their native language, the reopening of the four-centuries-old Hungarian Bolyai University in Cluj (Kolozhvar), and proper legal measures against those responsible for the anti-Hungarian massacres in Targu Mures (Marosvasarhely) in March of 1990.

In ideological terms, this means that "what Hungarians are demanding is the restoration of cultural, linguistic, and educational rights within Rumania. These are rights that Rumania has already guaranteed, on paper, to its national minorities as signatory to the UN human rights covenants and the Helsinki Final Act."[48] Unfortunately these international documents are highly flawed from a strict philosophical point of view. (For example, alongside civil and political rights, which are traditionally known as "negative" rights or rights requiring that people be left alone, the United Nations covenants also include so-called "economic rights" requiring the "positive" provision of goods or services by someone else.)[49] Yet politically these documents offer a useful device to press for the rights of minorities in an atmosphere colored by the deep hatred and intolerance evidenced in the newly formed Greater Romania Party.

The dilemma facing the minorities in Romania was succinctly and cogently summarized by sociologist Nicolae Gheorghe, a distinguished leader of the Romani (Gypsy) community, on June 13, 1991 at a conference on the nationality question sponsored by the Washington-based Institute of Peace: "The problem is that the Romanian government opposes the idea of 'collective rights.' While I and others realize that our ideal is the promotion of individual rights, respect for each individual equally before the law and a democratic system, we have questions about how to pursue this goal strategically." It is indeed a difficult choice, a problem with no clear solution. At the moment, the Gypsy community has been focusing on organizing political, social, and cultural institutions, as well as publishing bilingual newspapers such as *Aven Amentza/Veniti cu Noi (Come with Us)*.[50]

Since neo-Communism is still entrenched in Romania—with power remaining in centralized hands, privatization just barely begun, and civil society still in embryonic form—the Hungarian community has understandably opted for embracing the concept of "collective rights." For the moment at least, the state will continue to control vital resources: money for education, access to television, supplies of paper, and channels of distribution for most publications. Inevitably, therefore, the ethnic conflicts will have to play themselves out in the public arena. There is little doubt that the sooner the public arena shrinks and the private sector develops, the better for minorities—and for majorities as well.

The newly formed Civic Alliance, which was created on November 7, 1990, and which branched into a political party in mid-July 1991, is dedicated to equal rights and a Western-style democratic system, which necessarily implies respect for all individuals, and minorities in particular. For it is clear that without such respect there will not be a future for Romania.

The leader of the Civic Alliance party, literary critic Nicolae Manolescu, now editor of *Romania Literara (Literary Romania),* notes that "the 'nationalists' are no less hostile to liberalism than the communists. The national state, indeed at its extreme the ethnocentric state, can exhibit tribal and peasant elements but in no case can it be a liberal democracy. . . . The nationalists speak not of my right as an individual to liberty and justice, but only of my right as a Romanian to have a state able to protect me against external aggression."[51] From the point of view of political evolution, this is an essentially premodern conception. Manolescu's description of it as "tribal" graphically captures its primitive, not to say savage, quality.

The Civic Alliance follows in the spirit of Timisoara, the cradle of the December revolution, a multi-ethnic town where the spirit of pluralist cooperation is alive and well. Gheorghe Serban, president of the Timisoara Society believes that "what the people of Timisoara have in common is one week of fighting during which we were all together: workers, intellectuals, men, women, Romanians, Hungarians, Germans. We all saw the tanks, the bullets, the dead and mutilated bodies. . . . [I]t was the only place psychologically ready for a revolution. Because here we all had a sense of history. We always knew we belonged to Europe—that we were once at its center—and we resented being cut off from it."[52]

This sense of history has been recaptured, leaving an indelible impression. And unless the forces of hatred win out and cut off Romania once more from civilization there is a good chance that this nation will once more return to Europe, perhaps even to its center.

But it will not be easy. For in the first place Romanians will have to come to grips with the hostilities they feel toward each other. And they will have to overcome the temptation to be selective about their past. Writes Vasile Popovici, founder of the Timisoara Society:

> If we do have an identity, it is absurd for us to find it only in the Middle Ages or at the dawn of modernity or in the purest figures the Romanian people could create. . . . We [thought] the nationalist lie had died with the one who had forced [the Romanian] people to love itself through idiotic hymns and a gun at its head. But lo and behold, this lie continues to live on in a manner that makes us doubt ourselves once again.[53]

5. Overcoming the Spirit of *Miorita*

One of the most popular ballads of Romania, called *Miorita*, offers an interesting example of the idiosyncratic spirit of Romanians. It is a nostalgic, lyrical, tragic story about three shepherds—a Moldavian, a Transylvanian, and a Vrancean—the first being warned by his lamb Miorita that the other two are going to kill him because he is wealthy and has more sheep. The doomed man's response is to ask the lamb to tell the other two to bury him in the meadows near his sheep, so that he may be near his beloved woods, the birds, the stars. He then asks the lamb to urge everyone not to speak of death but rather to tell everyone— especially his teary-eyed mother who will be looking for him— that he has married a prince's daughter at heaven's gate.

It is a beautiful poetic story, whose main thrust is a profound love of nature and a stoical acceptance of destiny. Yet beyond this, the reader is struck by several other—moral—factors. In the first place, there is the appalling idea that two men plot to kill a richer one and the latter makes absolutely no effort to resist, accepting it as an inevitable course of destiny. Absent is any sense of justice, any need for vengeance, or any demand for retribution.

In one respect, therefore, the spirit of *Miorita* appears to be quite positive: a Christian sense of peace and lack of rancor. Yet one is reminded of the quiet passivity during the Ceausescu era, when the Romanian people accepted their fate without apparent turmoil. Is this the answer to Romania's current problems—a sense of great forgiveness on the part of those who may have been wronged? A sense of metaphysical tranquility, a love of nature, the simple things in life?

Not if this means, in fact, a false serenity: for surely it is only human to feel rage against injustice. Nor should one so readily accept "fate"; rather, one should seek to affect the course of history—for that is the path to a healthy sense of control and self-esteem. But above all there should be no deception about reality. The Moldavian shepherd who is the intended victim of his less wealthy "friends" tells the lamb to convey a pretty but inaccurate story.

This will not do. The Romanian people, if they are to overcome hostilities against each other—whether ethnic or social (or a combination of both)—will have to retrieve a sense of justice, which implies meting out punishment when this is feasible, as well as a sense of control over their destinies. This implies an optimism based not on illusion and lies but on self-assurance and truth. There will still be plenty of room for the profound sense of unity with nature, with the beautiful Romanian countryside.

Until it is no longer accepted that someone who is richer (or poorer, as in the case of the Gypsies), or speaks another language, or has different rituals—having nevertheless violated no one's rights—should be killed, indeed that someone who is unsuspecting, a friend, should be so treacherously deceived, the Romanian people have no future.

IV

Some Notes on Harmony

1. Anglo-American Footnotes

Why comb history for a clue to the concept of nationalism? Is there any point in seeking a bird's-eye view of this complex idea that has served many disparate purposes in radically different political circumstances? Is it not sheer self-deception to try to find a common denominator instead of becoming reconciled to the idea that "nationalism" is a term denoting a family of deceptively related concepts?

While on the one hand it is indeed impossible to conceive of an "essence" that somehow captures the idea in Platonic fashion, there is one important reason to study the concept that should assist in understanding the situation that obtains today in East-Central Europe and Romania in particular. That reason is simply the fact that some form of virulent "nationalism" is likely to replace Communism as the next ideology of authoritarianism should democracy fail in that region. Moreover, the pejorative connotations of the concept of "nationalism," combined with a positive aura, render it a particularly volatile tool whose ambiguity is manipulable for both good and evil. Thus, a look at the history of the concept helps us appreciate the existence of both the negative and the positive aspects, preparing us better for the ensuing danger. And conceptual clarity is essential in the complex political situation of the post-Communist era.

One issue that particularly vexes the newly liberated democracies is how to reconcile the concept of individual human rights with that of "ethnic collective rights." Are they, indeed, in conflict, or is a reconciliation possible? Addressing the question adequately is not easy, for it is necessary to remember the Marxist background against which the discussion takes place, and the damage that has been done by the tortured language and inhuman political straitjacket imposed by this system. For nearly five decades, the common vocabulary of East-Central Europe has consisted of that vulgar Hegelian oxymoron, "dialectical materialism." While the East-Central European guinea pigs who were subjected to the Marxist experiment have roundly and irrevocably repudiated Marxism in its entirely, it may be that even some of its relatively positive qualities—distorted as they were beyond recognition—have caused great revulsion.

To be specific, there is certainly one interesting, and probably not disingenuous, liberal element in *The Communist Manifesto* (which also appeared in Marx's early works): the predicated eventual dissolution of the state. This grain of quasi-liberalism, however, comes with a cruel twist: first man's nature is to be thoroughly, demonically transformed. Man is to be stripped of personal property and hence, presumably, of any egoistic inclinations. "Socialist man" must become blissfully amnesic with regard to his cultural and ethnic heritage. Then, deprived of all "classes" and conflict-causing associations, he will finally be worthy of the Marxist nirvana. At that point, there is no more need for a state. Yet neither, alas—it would seem—for life itself.

In brief, while each man is completely free to act as he wishes in the Marxist utopia, his wishes have become lobotomized; he is no longer human, but a mere cipher. What East-Central Europeans saw, to their horror, was the requirement for attaining such a presumed paradise. And they recoiled, terrified, stunned

—inoculated perhaps against all liberalisms, whether bogus or genuine. They became cynical: if this be limited government, forget it. The price is not worth it, for the price is everything.

But the Marxist post-totalitarian anarchy of robots is too obviously a caricature of liberalism. It must not be permitted to alienate the people of East-Central Europe from all healthy pluralism. It must be possible to rediscover the philosophical roots of the true liberal state and its ideal of limited government, which allows each individual to pursue his rights. Those rights involve one's dignity and identity, one's freedom of action. To paraphrase the popular joke that the difference between capitalism and socialism is the difference between a chair and an electric chair, classical liberalism allows man to sit comfortably, not mutilate his anatomy to mechanical dimensions. By analogy, the difference between the liberal limited state on the one hand, and the automatic order of automata predicted by Marx on the other, is frankly the difference between symphony and cacophony. They both involve sound, but the former is organic, the latter repulsive. Let me explain by turning, however briefly, to American classical-liberal theory.

The quintessential text that captures this theory is Thomas Jefferson's eloquent Declaration of Independence of 1776, which places the individual at the center of the moral universe. This does not imply a narrow, simple-minded egoism. To say that man is the locus of individual rights is mainly to deny that states—kings, presidents, or oligopolies—bestow rights upon their helpless subjects, who would otherwise be mere specks of dust. These rights are also sometimes called "natural" to indicate that they exist by virtue of man's very nature, that they are God-given or conforming to the laws of nature—God having created these laws according to reason. It follows that one discovers the existence of these rights by reason, which is deemed universal in all men. Put differently, man has rights in virtue of his existence as such, by virtue of his being endowed by his creator with the faculty of reason, *not* because he happens to have been born in any particular place or time. Those rights are simple enough to grasp: life, liberty, and property (or the means to pursue one's liberty—in Jefferson's words, "the pursuit of happiness"). Indeed, they can all be reduced to this one fundamental right: the right to liberty. Every human being must respect the existence, and space of action, of every other. The purpose of legitimate legislation, in turn, is not to hinder but actually to enhance liberty. Government is *by* the governed *for* the governed, with equal rights for all. And contrary to Marx, for the governed as they are, not as they may become.

Philosopher John Locke (1632-1704), Jefferson's mentor, had earlier explained this outlook in *The Second Treatise on Civil Government* in 1690. Living in the atmosphere of the Newtonian revolution in science, at a time when men were sure that the universe was beautifully ordered by a deity whose works could be understood by unaided reason, Locke expressed the belief that all men are equal under God. And they associate not to hurt each other but to reach a harmonious, prosperous existence, with each respecting each other's rights. He thus explained in his *Treatise*:

> [T]he end of law is not to abolish or restrain but to preserve and enlarge freedom; for in all the states of created beings, where there is no law, there is no freedom. For liberty is to be free from restraint and violence from others, which cannot be where there is no law; but freedom is not, as we are told: a liberty for every man to do what he lists—for who could be free, when every man's humor might domineer over him?—but a liberty to dispose and order as he lists his person, action, possessions, and his whole property, within the allowance of those laws under which he is, and therein not to be subject to the arbitrary will of another, but freely follow his own.[1]

Nor is it necessary to believe in God to appreciate the wisdom of equal liberty, but only to believe in order, and reason—without which common human action is impossible in any case.

The purpose of law, then, is actually to preserve and even enhance freedom: this is the *raison d' etre* of a healthy political system. Being free of violence, so as to pursue one's own ends unafraid, in concert with others if one wishes—that is the purpose of government. But notice what freedom is *not*: doing anything one wishes, whether or not it interferes with the rights of others. On the contrary, freedom involves limits: one may not violate others' legitimate rights to their own actions and property. And just as a man may not harm another (by murdering, stealing, or otherwise depriving him of what is his), neither may a government harm its subjects. It has no *right* to do so.

As Locke writes later in the same *Treatise*: "[P]olitical power is that power which every man having in the state of nature has given up into the hands of the society and therein to the governors whom the society has set over itself"—with a clear proviso that it "cannot be an absolute arbitrary power over their lives and fortunes." On the contrary, political power must "preserve the members of that society in their lives, liberties, and possessions."[2] The presumption of original power, that is, lies with the individual citizens. States derive their rights from the consent of the governed: states may do only what the subjects allow them to do and no more. It follows that states must not interfere with the peaceful pursuits of their subjects. And those pursuits can be virtually anything the subjects wish to pursue, within the limits of mutual tolerance.

It follows that whatever a man does voluntarily, without interfering with the rights of others to do the same—whatever associations he wishes to form, ethnic groups, language, and forms of ritual—governments cannot rightfully prohibit. Not only freedom of speech but freedom of religion and ethnic education are thereby guaranteed. So long as he respects others, a man must be allowed to act freely.

A century and a half later, in 1858, John Stuart Mill (1806-1873) explained with classic clarity in his essay *On Liberty*: if a man "refrains from molesting others in what concerns them, and merely acts according to his own inclination and judgment in things which concern himself, the same reasons which show that opinion should be free prove also that he should be allowed, without molestation, to carry his opinions into practice at his own cost."[3]

It might be argued, however, that the British condition is not particularly relevant to the nations emerging from post-Communist rubble: modern England is, after all, a rather homogeneous society, no model for the ethnic cauldron that is East-Central Europe. And perhaps so. Yet the same cannot be said of the United States, a diverse nation that has accommodated people from all over the world with remarkable resilience. And the United States has been governed for over two hundred years by what is essentially a classical-liberal perspective.

Not that the history of America has been strife-free. Certainly there have been racial, religious, and ethnic tensions. The European immigrants slaughtered much of the native Indian populations. But later, however inadequately, reservations were instituted to save whatever was left of Indian culture. A civil war was fought over the obscenity of slavery. It was won, however, by the side that championed extending rights to all men, irrespective of color. Without denying the continued existence of bigotry and injustice, the framework of tolerance has been surprisingly, spectacularly effective in the United States. That framework was established not only in the Declaration of Independence but also—most important—in the American Constitution, including its first ten amendments known as the Bill of Rights.

Throughout the country's history, orators have emerged to articulate *the principle of tolerance* that is responsible for the success of the American experiment. Consider this example from the last century, regarding discrimination on the basis of religion. In 1819, Judge Henry M. Brackenridge delivered a moving speech supporting repeal of an old Maryland law that forbade Jews to practice law or hold elective office: "Our political compacts are not entered into as brethren of the Christian faith," said Brackenridge, "but as men, as members of a civilized society. In looking back to our struggle for independence, I find that we engaged in that bloody conflict for THE RIGHTS OF MAN, and not for the purpose of enforcing or defending any particular religious creed."[4] This did not seem obvious to everyone; efforts to repeal that law failed until 1825, when arguments based on reason and the Constitution prevailed.

The speech by Judge Brackenridge could have been written today, and it might have been delivered in the parliament of, say, Romania—relevant to a debate regarding, for example, the rights of its Hungarian or Jewish minorities. Surely the concept that men are to be respected as such, irrespective of their historical background and the method of their worship, is relevant. Admittedly, this will require forgetting past wrongs, and tolerating differences. Perhaps it is emotionally too much to ask, after all the pain suffered in the recent past. But what is the alternative? Perpetuating hatred, and sitting in a political minefield.

The concept that associations ought to be fostered, whether they be religious, economic, or political, is absolutely essential to a free society. John Stuart Mill captured well the desirability of cultural, aesthetic, and other organic human groupings, directly contradicting the Marxist anti-utopia of forcibly fabricated "socialist man." "It is not by wearing down into uniformity all that is individual in themselves," writes Mill in the essay *On Liberty*, "but by cultivating it and calling it forth, within the limits imposed by the rights and interests of others, that human beings become a noble and beautiful object of contemplation," for "by the same process human life also becomes rich, diversified, and animating."[5] National identity is surely an important expression of colorful individuality, through the extension of one's cultural context. Pluralism adds nobility and diversity to the tapestry of human endeavor. Far from wishing to suppress such diversity, classical liberalism only wishes to limit its expression within the confines of civil society and prohibit its imposition through the state.

From a practical point of view, it is impossible to expect the nations of East-Central Europe to effect immediately a complete radical transition from totalitarian control to civil society. It will not do simply to say, for example, that Romania ought to allow Hungarians to run their own schools: where will the money come from, at the outset, when all education has been state-run for nearly five decades, and most people have no personal property? In the beginning, therefore, the problems of allocation of public funds to different national groups will be formidable.

Minorities throughout East-Central Europe will be in need of special assistance and special considerations. These problems of transition will require sensitivity on the part of legislators and special understanding on the part of majorities. It is important to remember, however, where this should all lead, and that ultimately the problems will be solved only when government gets out of the way, when individuals are allowed to pursue their own goals with their own resources, unhindered by bureaucrats.

2. Toward an East-Central European Classical Liberalism

However strong liberalism may be in the Anglo-American tradition, it is certainly not the exclusive province of the English-speaking people. What is more, both the colonizing English and the democratically inclined Americans have shown a tendency toward proselytizing, "civilizing," and absorbing "lesser" cultures. (The Americans, critics would argue, have shown this tendency to a fault.) The fact that America is "a melting pot," however positive in legal and economic terms, must give pause to the ethnic societies of East-Central Europe, whose experience under Communism dampened any desires to melt in any cauldron, no matter how benign. For these societies, liberalism must be accompanied by the most sophisticated and serious commitment to cultural vitality if it has any hope of adoption.

That commitment is to be found, eloquently and cogently defended, in the work of Austrian economist and philosopher Ludwig von Mises, who in his 1919 book *Nation, State, and Economy: Contributions to the Politics and History of Our Time* argued not only that freedom is thoroughly compatible with nationalism, but that the two are intrinsically connected.

Von Mises cherished pluralism and difference, the blend of cultures that has traditionally made the Danubian region a mosaic no less splendid than it is varied, however scarred by strife. He was a strong proponent of nationality (or nationalism), which he took to be an individualistic idea and opposed to "the collectivist idea of the racial community."[6] Nationality is based on a common language and thus on a similar cultural tradition as well. Far from believing that modernity and economic efficiency require the suppression of national differences, von Mises felt rather that the nationality principle was—or should be—entirely positive. Nationalism is predicated on the idea that freedom allows creativity and the development of one's ethnic heritage in any manner desired by the individual. But that applies to all nationalities, and all individuals. Thus, nationalism is to be fostered, for it "bears no sword against members of other nations. It is directed *in tyrannos*. . . . The idea of freedom is both national and cosmopolitan" at the same time.[7]

In brief, von Mises defended nationality because he believed in freedom. He thus appealed to the positive roots in the history of Western European nationalism:

> The Germans, the Italians became nationally minded because foreign princes, joined in the Holy Alliance, hinder them from . . . establishing a free state. This nationalism directs itself not against foreign peoples but against the despot who subjugates foreign peoples also.[8]

Thus, political and economic liberalism are exactly alike in proclaiming the solidarity of interests among peoples, that is, among nations: "as a political ideal [the national principle] is just as compatible with the peaceful coexistence of people as Herder's nationalism as a cultural ideal was compatible with cosmopolitanism."[9]

Which brings us back to the origins of East-Central European nationalism. Von Mises had much sympathy for the oppressed people of the former Hapsburg Empire. He was also highly critical of the protectionist and militarist tendencies of German and Russian conservatives, whom he criticized for fighting "against the ideas of freedom with the argument that they were foreign things not suitable for their peoples."[10] This elitism is wrong and politically motivated.

The only moral (and, coincidentally, most prudent) policy, argued von Mises, is individual freedom, which implies tolerance. Not only is freedom necessary for prosperity, it is necessary for the preservation of freedom itself. All other roads, whatever their apparent value, lead not only to serfdom and penury but to various forms of oppression, to the violation of human—which is to say, individual—rights. And such rights require minimal interference by the state.

For all other measures are bound to fail. Von Mises thus fully, and commendably, realized the limits of the democratic principle in polyglot, multinational states, for it leads to rule by majorities. This means that members of national minorities that do not hold a ruling position, who are not given a share in governing, are bound to consider themselves politically unfree, "political pariahs who have no say when matters concerning them are being debated."[11] Yet von Mises definitely felt that "proportional representation is no way out of these difficulties"—it provides only an illusory, highly flawed pseudo-solution. For "a minority is politically collaborating in the true sense of the word only if its voice is heard because it has prospects of coming to the helm some time. For a national minority, however, that is ruled out."[12] It is for this reason that the satisfactory solution to ethnic conflict—admitting that such conflict can never be completely obliterated, human nature being what it is—can only lie in limiting the size of government.

Hence von Mises's thoroughly liberal conclusion.

> The greater the scope the state claims in the life of the individual and the more important politics becomes for him, the more areas of friction are thereby created in territories with mixed population. Limiting state power to a minimum, as liberalism sought, would considerably soften the antagonisms between different nations that live side by side in the same territory. The only true national autonomy is the freedom of the individual against the state and society.[13]

How ironic that this should be the desideratum prescribed for a region that has been plagued with statist nationalism (as indicated in section 2 of Chapter II)—a region that distorted the humanist nationalism of Johann Herder into an exclusivist, mythical, xenophobic, and narcissistic ethnophilia. Worse yet (as elaborated in section 1 of that chapter), these people are just emerging from a traumatic anti-cultural experiment, tired and impoverished, psychologically ill-equipped for the tolerance that Enlightenment philosophers had in mind for the most civilized stage of human existence.

Perhaps it is indeed too much to ask. On the other hand, the American settlers who eventually opted for an exemplary Bill of Rights had also emerged from a long voyage across a treacherous ocean, most of them having landed on the soil of the New World with little more than a bundle of clothes. Subsequently, others joined them similarly ill-equipped. And they rose to the occasion, seizing the opportunity of freedom.

What is more, the people of East-Central Europe have gained at least one thing in the process of their exposure to the brutality of the Nazis and then the Marxist-Leninist utopia: experience. They have learned the dangers of ideologies that proclaim collectivist ideals at the expense of individual freedom. It is thus no accident that the work of one of Ludwig von Mises's most famous students, Friedrich Hayek (winner of the 1974 Nobel prize in economics), has been so influential.

In *The Road to Serfdom*, first published in 1944 and disseminated underground throughout East-Central Europe during the Communist occupation,[14] Hayek wrote that collectivism of all stripes is intrinsically anti-democratic:

> It may indeed be questioned whether anyone can realistically conceive of a collectivist program other than in the service of a limited group, whether collectivism can exist in any form other than that of some kind of particularism, be it nationalism, racialism, or classism.[15]

This applies, to be specific, both to Marxism and National Socialism. Hayek was convinced that the root of evil is "that glorification of power which easily leads from socialism to nationalism and which profoundly affects the ethical views of all collectivists. So far as the rights of small nations are concerned, Marx and Engels were little better than most other consistent collectivists, and the views occasionally expressed about Czechs and Poles resemble those of contemporary National Socialists."[16]

Distrust of particularism as a political form is the philosophical leap that allows a repudiation of all forms of antiliberalism. To make this leap is to take a road forever away from serfdom. This, it seems, many of the people in East-Central Europe have learned, very much the hard way.

There is little doubt that this is so, in theory. But can it be done in practice? Will East-Central Europe—and Romania in particular—be able to embrace freedom? Returning to pluralism seems too exhausting. There is so much felt hurt, and where is one to turn if not to government? Above all, the priorities are confused: what should be salvaged first? One's individual identity or one's ethnic heritage? Should one look out for oneself and one's family, one's national group, or one's country, first?

Perhaps reform should start with semantics. One useful linguistic suggestion is to assiduously attempt to avoid the use of the term "nationalism" altogether whenever possible. In its place, such concepts as "tradition," "patriotism," "national identity," "ethnic identity," and many others can be used to capture the term's positive connotations. If the negative connotations are intended, there are plenty of terms to choose from: "xenophobia," "ethnocentrism," "chauvinism," and "racism" will do well. The main goal is to separate the negative from the positive as clearly as possible so as to avoid vagueness and ambiguity that leads to dangerous misunderstanding and confusing euphemism. Above all, there is danger in using the positive connotations of a term to provide justification for negative ends. Thus, "nationalism" must never be invoked to lend credibility to what are purely hate-filled or opportunistic tactics.

The post-Communist era is particularly vulnerable to the manipulation of language. Marxism-Leninism reached unprecedented heights in bending language to the point of complete distortion to mask the most repressive and cruel system in history. "Freedom" was used to excuse total control; "democracy" masked the lack of any electoral choice; it should not surprise us that the practice of over four decades has made some people experts in the art of linguistic deception. "Nationalism" is obviously the top candidate for manipulation at a time when the nations of East-Central Europe seek to redefine their identities. Invoking it will excuse many dangerous practices. What is worse, those who seem to oppose it are made to look evil and unpatriotic. To repeat: the best linguistic solution is avoiding the term.

Not that it will be possible at all times. The word is here to stay. But calling attention to its drawbacks is at least a start.

Flagging it as a probable red herring may at least sensitize the audience to its possible misuse, to likely mischief.

Ultimately, beyond linguistic decisions there will have to be political safeguards for true pluralism. What this means is the kind of constitutional framework that protects the rights of all men as provided, for example, by the American Bill of Rights. This series of amendments to the constitution further cements the principle, firmly embodied in that document, that government is constituted to protect rights that men already have by nature; the rights are not created by state decree. An independent judiciary, moreover, is absolutely essential to defend the individual against state abuse.

Exactly the wrong approach is the one taken by the new Romanian Constitution ratified by the Parliament at the close of 1991. This Constitution starts out by declaring Romania to be a "unitary" state. This statement has been widely understood to imply intolerance; it has been seen as an attempt to outlaw such opposition parties as the Hungarian Democratic Union, the largest opposition party represented in Parliament today. In other words, the current Romanian Constitution appears to be intended to codify the worst aspects of nationalism.

Article 6 specifically deals with national minorities and what is termed their "right to [a separate national] identity." Section 1 of the article stipulates that the state "recognizes and guarantees the right of conservation, development, and expression of ethnic, cultural, linguistic, and religious identity for persons belonging to national minorities." Section 2 of the same article, however, negates much of this by denying national minorities any collective rights. Another seeming contradiction appears in Article 13, which specifically stipulates that the official language is Romanian. Generally, the Romanian Constitution is an uneasy mixture of desiderata that may be read very differently, indeed contradictorily, by different constituencies.

This will not do. A solid legal footing is indispensable for the country to start along the path of reform. Unless Romania implements a system of individual freedom, it will reach neither prosperity nor political respectability, and its citizens will continue to seek emigration in droves as they do today. The revolution appears not to be quite over. Unfortunately, a child growing up in Romania learns that the red in his nation's tricolor flag stands for blood; this may continue to be true.

We are currently witnessing hard times in East-Central Europe. There is much to be overcome, both intellectually and emotionally. For nearly five decades, the people have been pawns in a zero-sum game. To help oneself one had to break the law and defy the official line about what is good for the country. The people have suffered systematic, hypocritical, effective violations of every conceivable human right at the hands of an unelected, Marxist-Leninist mafia. Moreover, they have been denied access to literature explaining the concept of natural rights. As a result, it is no wonder there is conceptual confusion. Yet it seems to me that the classical-liberal model provides the most logical way out of the current impasse—the fastest, most effective way for East-Central Europe to join the rest of the civilized world.

This does not mean that the way out is either theoretically transparent or within immediate, easy reach. But it is worth a try. For on closer examination, it will become clear that many problems are avoidable: that one can pursue one's interests and at the same time not betray one's national heritage—while indeed respecting the heritage of others as well.

The greatest Hungarian lyric poet of the twentieth century, Endre Ady (1877-1919), spoke well for the common interests of the people in his region of the world: "For a thousand years the sorrow of the Magyars, the Slavs, and the Wallachs has been the same sorrow. They are kindred peoples. Why can they not come together on the barricades of the spirit?"[17] Why not indeed? Let them gather together under the flag of fraternity and equality before a God who must have had a reason for creating them all. Their sorrow has already gone on much too long.

Afterword:

Subterranean Societies

by Vasile Popovici *

An immense region inhabited by dozens of peoples, stretching all the way from the Berlin Wall (when it was still intact) to the eastern shore of Asia, feverishly seeks its equilibrium, after such a lengthy and unnatural situation. And it would be a grave mistake not to notice that Communism is not the only thing responsible for the historic drama we are currently undergoing. Before or alongside Communism, Europe has known the hysteria of nationalism. Whether under the nationalists or the Communists, we have seen the only order that an exclusivist ideology could create: the military order.

---

* This article was published in Romanian as "Societatile Din Subterana" in *Meridian*, vol. 1, no. 4 (November-December 1991), and is reprinted by permission. Translated by Juliana Geran Pilon.

Vasile Popovici, the founder of the Timisoara Society—an organization dedicated to the principles of the revolution, notably pluralism and openness—teaches French literature at the University of Timisoara. He also manages the West Publishing House and has been published in literary magazines both in Romania and abroad.

Beyond utopias that are equally criminal, beyond their succes-
sive—and often quite obvious—deaths, something survives intact: the military spirit and, together with it, a system of values
based on force, intolerant and violent. The totalitarian societies
took the barrack as a model and took militarism as a civil norm.

When everything appears to be collapsing in our part of the
world, the hard nucleus that served with equal fervor both
Nazism and Communism offers itself as a solution. With brutal
yet apparently effective primitivism, it starts again and proposes
the same old—always handy—solution of nationalist chauvinism which suits it so naturally. This time it is the turn of generalized hatred: everyone against everyone. Wedded to misery
and desperation, the military mentality is now in full swing,
completely, desperately free.

Communism has run out of resources, even in Romania, but
it is highly improbable that its only alternative is democracy.
Much more likely is the Yugoslav version, which is only a more
advanced stage of a reality that presents a very real threat. And
the first step toward a generalized Yugoslavia, from Budapest to
Vladivostok, is the exacerbation of nationalism.

Democracy has its own demands that suffering and want
cannot satisfy. The military spirit, however, feeds on little: collective self-exaltation (nationalism) and the invention of the
ethnic Enemy (chauvinism) are enough to satisfy it. Both conditions are always at its disposal. When given discretionary
powers, it has changed borders, homogenized and displaced
enormous masses of people from one region to another, and
gutted any act of self-assertion. Now the center has lost power,
but its spirit persists everywhere. What we have inherited from
the center, the military mentality, has combined with the will to
attain ethnic freedom outside of any democratic norms. The
result is an aggressive nationalism, determined to obtain everything *now*, in spite of everyone.

Nationalism, almost always aggravated by chauvinism, is the
fundamental problem of post-Communist societies—and I do

not for a moment forget the importance of the economic question. But we can imagine the most promising economic plans
possible, we can obtain credits, we can privatize and liberalize,
no matter. Any effort is doomed to failure from the outset if we
do not find a formula to survive without destroying one another.
It appears, however, that neither our societies, which are much
too deeply caught in a current that pushes us in a dangerous
direction, nor, unfortunately, the West, realize the force and
gravity of the phenomenon.

The force of nationalism rests in its dual nature, both instinctual and intellectual. It always has a content: the representation of
an ethnic group to itself, creating an image with which the group
identifies and which facilitates its self-aggrandizement. Is there a
national identity? Is there a basis for the national sentiment, in
other words? Undoubtedly not, if we seek the answer in the
realm of metaphysics: if we seek an "essence" of the collective
spirit once and for all.

There is, however, a national identity in an uninterrupted
process of creation following the accidents of history and the
accidental works of the individual creative spirit; prestige and
time transform these accidents into a common value. It is a
process that presupposes selectivity. What specifically does a
people select from its history, from its culture? What specifically
does it consider to be *representative* of itself? Here there is much
room for deceit and self-flattery. Like any narcissistic image,
this too is heavily laden with subconscious energy.

Among the intellectual values recognized as "national" and the
background energy of collectivities that is always available and
inflammable, there is a potentially open channel of communication. Stated differently, this instinctual energy may be
explosively freed at certain moments, particularly when the
collectivities are upset, challenged in their self-perception. And,
after all, the departure from Communism involves a difficult
process of reversing a long period of utter humiliation. For
dozens of years, half of the peoples of Europe had lived on their

knees. Even when—as in the Russian Empire—the people had a feeling of power, it still lived on its knees. This humiliation is now seeking revenge.

While the national sentiment has become over the course of two centuries a real, present sentiment (it has not been here "since the beginning of time," being a romantic acquisition, and not a naturally given fact), nationalism itself is a kind of excitation, an exaltation typical of exclusivism and hence totalitarianism. An analysis of the national identity may be legitimate, but *it is really meaningful* only if, with the assistance of scholarship, it uses *the critical spirit*.

Anyone will agree, however, that our society today is far from receptive to the conclusions of the critical spirit. Let's stop for a moment to look at what is happening in Romania. It is ever so instructive!

I believe that it is only fitting that we Romanians (and this goes for our neighbors too, by the way) should at last assume that whatever our culture and our history says about us is no less relevant—even if it is not particularly flattering—than the great achievements of popular culture, [the Romantic poet Mihail] Eminescu or the figure of [the medieval leader] Mihai the Brave.

During the last years of the most mendacious, most blatant and unbearable nationalist exaltation of the Ceausescu era, one portion of the Romanian intelligentsia has attempted to achieve a more lucid interpretation of our heritage by reminding us that the spirit of [the pre-Communist satirist playwright Ion Luca] Caragiale suits us better than that of Eminescu.

Caragiale exists, unquestionably, in our innermost being, but his treacherous and immoral world seems to us *today* rather like a festive world, a world of carnival, whose unconscious cruelty we aim toward as if it were a land of eternal peace. An all too flowery world, a world of operetta, distant and inaccessible. Meanwhile a thing or two has taken place: to our national fiber was added a pathetic component, and a murderous one.

That December when *our* leaders, the best of *our* criminals succeeded, moreover, to compromise everything in the eyes of the world, that December which even he [Ceausescu] made for us, we discovered our pathetic dimension: without weapons and without any orders, thousands of people risked their lives for freedom. And some even died.

This is, however, only one side of the coin. The other looks totally different. Those who pulled the trigger during those days, those who asked that the triggers be pulled, from Ceausescu to [General] Stanculescu [head of the Securitate, apparently responsible for the shootings in Timisoara, currently counselor to President Ion Iliescu] and from him to the last little army officer, whether Securitate or militia, were also Romanian. We must acknowledge them, too. They, too, are *ours*.

We were quick to make Ceausescu out as a Tatar, or a Gypsy. Anything but a Romanian. But we must acknowledge him too, as a shameful and self-aggrandizing Romanian stupidity. But we will have to descend even more deeply in our intimate misery to come to grips with Cornel Vadim Tudor['s *Great Romania*], the weekly prized by hundreds of thousands of our countrymen. Absolute vulgarity reverberates somewhere in our national being, if such obscenity can take up so much of the national scene.

Nothing authorizes us to select from the last fifty years, for example, [the writer] Marin Preda as typical. Not even if it is true that—confused by the nonsense of history, but admirable in his decision always to return to the force and lucidity of the rational spirit—his singular peasant lives the fate of an entire people of peasants. It seems to me that there is something much more representative than a conscience that does not give in: the endless multitude of consciences ready for any compromise.

If we do have an identity, it would be absurd to seek it only in the Middle Ages, or at the dawn of the modern epoch, or in the purest figures that the Romanian people has produced. We have the duty to take into account as well the last centuries and the last half of the present century, to which we have been witnesses, and performers. That there is too little glory and too much misery in this period must not discourage us: for it is like ourselves.

For many it was a big surprise to find, after the fall of Ceausescu, that the nationalist discourse still "works," that it sounds plausible even in the mouths of Securitate officers, who drape themselves in the national flag to offer us the supreme justification—and supreme contempt. We had thought then that the nationalist lie had died with the one who had forced his people to love itself through idiotic hymns and a gun at its head. But lo and behold, this lie continues to live on in a manner that makes us doubt ourselves once again, and still more.

A just trial would liberate us (perhaps) from ourselves, and it might (perhaps) give us what it takes to accept the Others: the Hungarians, Serbs, or Russians, themselves locked within their own nationalist lies.

Just as economic change requires first a political change, emerging from the underground requires a spiritual revival; it cannot come from the outside, no matter how great is the Western export of democratic values. We must acknowledge our subterranean existence, discuss it, and externalize our internal spiritual crisis.

In order not to devour each other, the subterranean societies have fought with the internal monster, always ready to admire themselves in the treacherous mirrors of nationalism. The more monstrous, the more decorated.

Appendix:

The Copenhagen Document

Since 1975, when the nations of East-Central Europe joined the Western Europeans, Canada, and the United States in signing the so-called Helsinki Accords or Helsinki Final Act, there has been a well-recognized international forum for the discussion and "enforcement" of human rights, in particular the rights of minorities or nationalities. At times this has meant that an illusion of legality soothed a guilty Western conscience, aware that it could do little to influence events behind the Iron Curtain. But at other times it worked: it turned out that East-Central European and Soviet dissidents used the Helsinki Final Act in ingenious and highly effective ways to press their demands for greater freedom.

With the demise of the Soviet bloc, the entire "Helsinki process" entered a new phase, and new problems appeared alongside some of the old ones. Human rights continued to need protection, even after the anti-Communist revolution. Meeting in Copenhagen from June 5 to 29, 1990, the signatories thus

97

agreed to a statement of common principles known as "The Copenhagen Document," which focuses on human rights issues ("the human dimension"). While not legally binding, this document offers some useful standards to which the signatory members can be legitimately held.

The following section, which is quoted here in full, constitutes Part IV of that document. It specifically relates to the question of national minorities. Some comments follow the citation.

* * *

Document of the Copenhagen Meeting of the Conference on the Human Dimension of the Conference on Security and Cooperation in Europe*

Part IV

The participating States recognize that the questions relating to national minorities can only be satisfactorily resolved in a democratic political framework based on the rule of law, with a functioning independent judiciary. This framework guarantees full respect for human rights and fundamental freedoms, equal rights and status for all citizens, the free expression of all their legitimate interests and aspirations, political pluralism, social tolerance and the implementation of legal rules that place effective restraints on the abuse of governmental power.

They also recognize the important role of non-governmental

---

* Washington: United States Government Printing Office, June 1990, part IV, pp. 16-20.

organizations, including political parties, trade unions, human rights organizations and religious groups, in the promotion of tolerance, cultural diversity and the resolution of questions relating to national minorities.

They further reaffirm that respect for the rights of persons belonging to national minorities as part of universally recognized human rights is an essential factor for peace, justice, stability and democracy in the participating States.

Persons belonging to national minorities have the right to exercise fully and effectively their human rights and fundamental freedoms without any discrimination and in full equality before the law.

The participating States will adopt, where necessary, special measures for the purpose of ensuring to persons belonging to national minorities full equality with the other citizens in the exercise and enjoyment of human rights and fundamental freedoms.

To belong to a national minority is a matter of a person's individual choice and no disadvantage may arise from the exercise of such choice.

Persons belonging to national minorities have the right freely to express, preserve and develop their ethnic, cultural, linguistic or religious identity and to maintain and develop their culture in all its aspects, free of any attempts at assimilation against their will. In particular, they have the right

— to use freely their mother tongue in private as well as in public;

— to establish and maintain their own educational, cultural and religious institutions, organizations or associations, which can seek voluntary financial and other contributions as well as public assistance, in conformity with national legislation;

— to profess and practice their religion, including the acquisition, possession and use of religious materials, and to conduct religious educational activities in their mother tongue;

— to establish and maintain unimpeded contacts among themselves within their country as well as contacts across frontiers with citizens of other States with whom they share a common ethnic or national origin, cultural heritage or religious beliefs;

— to disseminate, have access to and exchange information in their mother tongue;

— to establish and maintain organizations or associations within their country and to participate in international non-governmental organizations.

Persons belonging to national minorities can exercise and enjoy their rights individually as well as in community with other members of the group. No disadvantage may arise for a person belonging to a national minority on account of the exercise or non-exercise of any such rights.

The participating States will protect the ethnic, cultural, linguistic and religious identity of national minorities on their territory and create conditions for the promotion of that identity. They will take the necessary measures to that effect after due consultations, including contacts with organizations or associations of such minorities, in accordance with the decision-making procedures of each State.

Any such measures will be in conformity with the principles of equality and non-discrimination with respect to the other citizens of the participating State concerned.

The participating States will endeavour to ensure that persons belonging to national minorities, notwithstanding the need to learn the official language or languages of the State concerned, have adequate opportunities for instruction of their mother tongue or in their mother tongue, as well as, wherever possible and necessary, for its use before public authorities, in conformity with applicable national legislation.

In the context of the teaching of history and culture in educational establishments, they will also take account of the history and culture of national minorities.

The participating States will respect the right of persons belonging to national minorities to effective participation in public affairs, including participation in the affairs relating to the protection and promotion of the identity of such minorities.

The participating States note the efforts undertaken to protect and create conditions for the promotion of the ethnic, cultural, linguistic and religious identity of certain national minorities by establishing, as one of the possible means to achieve these aims, appropriate local or autonomous administrations corresponding to the specific historical and territorial circumstances of such minorities and in accordance with the policies of the State concerned.

The participating States recognize the particular importance of increasing constructive co-operation among themselves on questions relating to national minorities. Such co-operation seeks to promote mutual understanding and confidence, friendly and good-neighbourly relations, international peace, security and justice.

Every participating State will promote a climate of mutual respect, understanding, co-operation and solidarity among all persons living on its territory, without distinction as to ethnic or national origin or religion, and will encourage the solution of problems through dialogue based on the principles of the rule of law.

None of these commitments may be interpreted as implying any right to engage in any activity or perform any action in contravention of the purposes and principles of the Charter of the United Nations, other obligations under international law or the provisions of the Final Act, including the principle of territorial integrity of States.

The participating States, in their efforts to protect and promote the rights of persons belonging to national minorities, will fully respect their undertakings under existing human rights conventions and other relevant international instruments and consider adhering to the relevant conventions, if they have not yet done so, including those providing for a right of complaint by individuals.

The participating States will co-operate closely in the competent international organizations to which they belong, including the United Nations and, as appropriate, the Council of Europe, bearing in mind their on-going work with respect to questions relating to national minorities.

They will consider convening a meeting of experts for a thorough discussion of the issue of national minorities.

The participating States clearly and unequivocally condemn totalitarianism, racial and ethnic hatred, anti-semitism, xenophobia and discrimination against anyone as well as persecution on religious and ideological grounds. In this context, they also recognize the particular problems of Roma (Gypsies).

They declare their firm intention to intensify the efforts to combat these phenomena in all their forms and therefore will

— take effective measures, including the adoption, in conformity with their constitutional systems and their international obligations, of such laws as may be necessary, to provide protection against any acts that constitute incitement to violence against persons or groups based on national, racial, ethnic or religious discrimination, hostility or violence as a result of their racial, ethnic, cultural, linguistic, or religious identity, and to protect their property;

— take effective measures, in conformity with their constitutional systems, at the national, regional and local levels to promote understanding and tolerance, particularly in the fields of education, culture and information;

— endeavour to ensure that the objectives of education include special attention to the problem of racial prejudice and hatred and to the development of respect for different civilizations and cultures;

— recognize the right of the individual to effective remedies and endeavour to recognize, in conformity with national legislation, the right of interested persons and groups to initiate and support complaints against acts of discrimination, including racist and xenophobic acts;

— consider adhering, if they have not yet done so, to the international instruments which address the problem of discrimination and ensure full compliance with the obligations therein, including those relating to the submission of periodic reports;

— consider, also, accepting those international mechanisms which allow States and individuals to bring communications relating to discrimination before international bodies.

* * *

The result of negotiations and compromise, this is obviously not a flawless document. Some of the more obvious problems are:

1. The concept of a "national minority" is unclear. How is it to be distinguished, for example, from ethnic, linguistic, or religious minorities? What makes a minority "national"? Is it specific national(ist) claims?

2. Participating States will adopt "where necessary" special measures ensuring full equality with other citizens. But when is it necessary? Who decides?

3. Members of minorities are entitled to seek not only private but also "public assistance, in conformity with national legislation." But what if that legislation allows for virtually no such public assistance? Are there any principles to guide such legislation? And how will the majority react? What are the arguments to justify forcing them to provide such "public assistance," especially in the current tight economic situation?

4. Signatories to the Copenhagen Document will "create conditions for the promotion of [ethnic, cultural, linguistic, and religious] identity . . . [and will] take the necessary measures to that effect after due consultations" with minorities. What are such "due consultations"? Whom exactly will they involve? And what constitutes adequate "conditions" for the promotion of this national identity? There are no guidelines indicated.

5. "Wherever possible and necessary," everyone will be afforded the opportunity to use his mother tongue "before public authorities, in conformity with applicable national legislation." But when is it necessary? What determines the "possible"? Will the majority not balk at having to pay for this? Will their rights not be infringed by this "positive" duty?

6. "The principle of territorial integrity of States" is to be respected. But what if a national group decides to go off on its own, as has already been the case in Yugoslavia since the signing of the document, to say nothing of the Soviet republics? This phrase all but invites violation at this political junction.

On the other hand, there are also many positive features in this document.

1. As stated at the outset, questions relating to national minorities must take place within a democratic political framework based on the rule of law and necessarily require an independent judiciary.

2. The private sector is crucial in promoting tolerance and cultural diversity.

3. Minorities have the right to freely express themselves—this is simply an application of the universal concept of freedom.

4. There is a positive duty on the part of governments to combat "incitement to violence" based on anti-Semitism, xenophobia, and other forms of discrimination. This provision should make it more difficult for governments who might otherwise not only fail to combat such behavior but actually foster it.

5. There should be an effort made to promote respect for other minority groups. Such efforts are always welcome, and worth reinforcing.

The effectiveness of the Copenhagen Document is debatable. It proved powerless in preventing the crisis in Yugoslavia, for example. Indeed it may have fueled it, in light of the territorial inviolability clause that certainly seems to have forbidden Croatia's move to independence. It has also obviously failed to prevent the abuses in Romania mentioned above in Chapter III, section 3. But it does offer some useful signposts, and reminders. Paula Dobriansky, Associate Director for Programs at the U.S. Information Agency, who was involved in drafting the document, points out that it represents "the first time in the history of the Helsinki process that minority and nationality rights have been discussed specifically as such."

In particular, the very process of Helsinki points to the potential utility of a supranational organization to counteract nationalist and, potentially, autarkic tendencies. There appear to be many good reasons for the nations of East-Central Europe, including the Baltic republics as well as Turkey and Greece, to form a loose confederation designed to combat these noxious tendencies. In the interest of both economic and political liberalism, such a move seems welcome, if perhaps psychologically somewhat premature. The concept is certainly worth exploring.

Notes

Introduction

1. Vladimir Tismaneanu, *Reinventing Politics: Eastern Europe from Stalin to Havel* (New York, Toronto: The Free Press, 1992), p. 286.

2. Isaiah Berlin, *The Crooked Timber of Humanity: Chapters in the History of Ideas* (London and New York: Alfred A. Knopf, 1991), p. 245.

3. Gale Stokes in Occasional Paper Number 13 (Washington: Woodrow Wilson Center, July 1988), p. 23.

4. For a comprehensive though admittedly brief bibliography and discussion of major scholarly figures and theories, see Louis L. Snyder, *Encyclopedia of Nationalism* (New York: Paragon House, 1990).

Chapter I

1. Writes Nelson Goodman: "[S]ymbolization is an irrepressible propensity of man. . . . Art depends upon and helps sustain society— exists because, and helps ensure, that no man is an island." Nelson Goodman, *Languages of Art: An Approach to the Theory of Symbols* (Indianapolis, New York, Kansas City: Bobbs-Merrill, 1968), p. 257.

2. See Willard van Orman Quine, *Word and Object* (Cambridge: MIT Press, 1967), p. 13: "[E]ven the sophisticated learning of a new word is commonly a matter of learning it in context—hence learning,

by example and analogy, the usage of sentences in which the word can occur."

3. Eva Hoffman, *Lost in Translation: A Life in a New Language* (New York: E. P. Dutton, 1989), p. 209.

4. *Ibid.*, p. 107.

5. *Ibid.*, p. 108.

6. *Ibid.*

7. On German national feeling in the Middle Ages, see, for example, Herbert William Carruth, "The Expression of German National Feeling from the Middle of the Tenth Century to Walther von der Vogelwide," in *Harvard Studies and Notes in Philology and Literature,* vol. 2 (Boston: Ginn, 1893), pp. 127-54.

8. See, for example, Kamil Krofta, "L'Aspect national et social du mouvement Hussite," *Le Monde Slave*, vol. 5 (Paris, 1928), pp. 321-51.

9. See Esme Wingfield-Stratford, *The History of English Patriotism* (London: John Lane, 1913), vol. 1, p. 78.

10. See Carlton J. H. Hayes, *The Historical Evolution of Modern Nationalism* (New York: Macmillan, 1931), ch. 5, esp. pp. 120-33.

11. Hans Kohn, *Nationalism: Its Meaning and History* (New York: Van Nostrand Reinhold, 1965), p. 23.

12. Johann Gottfried von Herder, *Sammtliche Werke*, ed. Bernard Suphan (Berlin: Weidmann, 1877-1913), vol. 1, p. 2.

13. *Ibid.*, vol. 18, p. 237.

14. See Georg Schmidt-Rohr, *Die Sprache als Bilderin der Volker* (Jena: Diederichs, 1932).

15. See C. A. Macartney, *National States and National Minorities* (New York: Russell and Russell, 1968).

16. Robert Michels, *Notes sur les moyens de constater la nationalite* (Notes regarding ways to determine nationality) (The Hague: Martinus Nijhoff, 1917), p. 1.

17. Arnold J. Toynbee, *Nationality and the War* (London: J. M. Dent, 1915), p. 13.

18. See Hans Kohn, *The Idea of Nationalism: A Study in Its Origins and Background* (New York: Macmillan, 1944), pp. 7-8, for some specific examples.

19. Georg Wilhelm Friedrich Hegel, *Philosophy of History*, in

Great Books of the Western World, ed. Robert Maynard Hutchins (Chicago: University of Chicago Press, 1952), vol. 46, p. 177.

20. *Ibid.*

21. Hayes, *The Historical Evolution of Modern Nationalism* (see n. 10 above), p. 213.

22. Kohn, *The Idea of Nationalism*, p. 15.

23. See Niccolo Machiavelli, *The History of Florence Together with The Prince* (London: Bell and Daldy, 1972), esp. pp. 483-87.

24. *Ibid.*

25. E. J. Hobsbawm, *Nations and Nationalism Since 1780: Programme, Myth, Reality* (Cambridge: Cambridge University Press, 1991), p. 22: "The equation state = nation = people applied to both, but for the nationalists the creation of the political entities which would contain it derived from the prior existence of some community distinguishing itself from foreigners, while for the revolutionary-democratic point of view the central concept was the sovereign citizen-people = state which, in relation to the remainder of the human race, constitute a 'nation.' "

26. Cited in *The Dynamics of Nationalism: Readings in Its Meaning and Development*, ed. Louis L. Snyder (Princeton: D. Van Nostrand Co., 1964), p. 3.

27. "Where the sentiment of nationality exists in any force, there is a *prima facie* case for uniting all the members of the nationality under the same government." John Stuart Mill, "Representative Government," in *Great Books of the Western World*, ed. Robert Maynard Hutchins (Chicago: University of Chicago Press, 1952), vol. 43, ch. 16, p. 424.

28. *Ibid.*

29. V. I. Lenin, "Critical Remarks on the National Question," in *Collected Works of V. I. Lenin* (Moscow: Foreign Languages Publishing House, 1948), p. 37. ("Verst" is a Russian unit of length equal to roughly two thirds of a mile.)

30. For a thorough analysis of Lenin's contribution to Marxism—particularly the emphasis on a vanguard elite and the secondary nature of nationalism—see Leszek Kolakowski, *Main Currents of Marxism: Its Rise, Growth, and Dissolution*, vol. 2 (Oxford: Clarendon Press, 1978), esp. pp. 384-404.

31. It is important also to recognize that nationalism may be considered independently from nation and statehood. Thus, Anthony D. Smith notes that "there are many nationalisms without nations," offering by way of example the words of the famous Hungarian political figure Lajos Kossuth, who said in 1848 that "one nation can live under several different governments, and again several nations can form a single state." See Anthony D. Smith, *Theories of Nationalism* (London and Southampton: Camelot Press Ltd., 1971), p. 177.

32. Kohn, *The Idea of Nationalism* (see n. 18 above), p. 18.

33. An excellent bibliography of twentieth-century "Basic Books on Nationalism" may be found in *The Dynamics of Nationalism*, ed. Louis L. Snyder (see n. 26 above), pp. 377-78.

34. John Oakesmith, *Race and Nationality: An Inquiry into the Origin and Growth of Nationalism* (New York: Stokes, 1919).

35. Friedrich Otto Hertz, *Race and Civilization* (New York: Ktav Publishing House, 1970).

36. Florian Znaniecki, *Modern Nationalities: A Sociological Study* (Westport, Conn.: Greenwood Press, 1973).

37. Karl W. Deutsch, *Nationalism and Social Communication: An Inquiry into the Foundations of Nationality* (Cambridge: Technology Press of Massachusetts, 1953).

38. Smith, *Theories of Nationalism* (see n. 31 above), p. 191.

39. What makes the concept even more complicated is the fact that nationalities are not identical with other groups such as clans, tribes, and various folk-groups, sometimes called "ethnographic groups." See Kohn, *The Idea of Nationalism*, p. 13.

40. Kohn, *Nationalism: Its Meaning and History* (see n. 11 above), p. 11.

41. Robert Musil, "Essays 1918-1933," in *Precision and Soul* (Chicago: University of Chicago Press, 1990), p. 106.

42. Lord Acton, "Nationality," in *Essays on Freedom and Power* (Glouster, Mass.: P. Smith, 1972).

43. Elie Kedourie, *Nationalism* (London: Hutchinson University Library, 1960), p. 9.

44. Peter Sugar, "The Problems of Nationalism in Eastern Europe —Past and Present," Occasional Paper Number 13 (Washingon: Woodrow Wilson Center, July 1988), p. 4.

45. See, for example, Hayes, *The Historical Evolution of Modern Nationalism* (see n. 10 above), esp. pp. 232-41.

46. There is a rich literature on the subject. For example, see Barry Riddell's *Economic Nationalism* (Toronto: Maclean-Hunter, 1969). Specifically concerning Eastern Europe, see Leo Pasvolsky, *Economic Nationalism of the Danubian States* (New York: Johnson Reprint Corp., 1972).

47. Musil, "Essays 1918-1933" (see n. 41 above), p. 103.

48. Smith, *Theories of Nationalism* (see n. 31 above), p. 17.

49. Carlton J. H. Hayes, *Essays on Nationalism* (New York: Macmillan, 1926), p. 250.

50. K. R. Minogue, *Nationalism* (London: B. T. Batsford, Ltd., 1967) p. 79. See all of ch. 3 on "Nationalism and German Unity," pp. 53-80.

51. Sigmund Freud, "Thoughts for the Times on War and Death," in *Great Books of the Western World*, ed. Robert Maynard Hutchins (Chicago: University of Chicago Press, 1952), vol. 54, p. 761.

52. *Ibid.*

Chapter II

1. Cited in Michael Dobbs, "Nationalism Replacing Communism as Source of Instability," *The Washington Post*, October 27, 1991, p. A32.

2. *Ibid.*

3. Hugh Seton-Watson, *The Sick Heart of Europe: The Problem of the Danubian Lands* (Seattle: University of Washington Press, 1975).

4. See for example Robert Lee Wolf, *The Balkans in Our Time* (New York: W. W. Norton & Co., 1967), ch. 15, sections 2 and 3.

5. *Ibid.*, p. 575.

6. Vaclav Havel et al., *The Power of the Powerless* (Armonk, N.Y.: M. E. Sharpe, Inc., 1990), pp. 36-37.

7. See Juliana Geran Pilon, "From Kafka to Hayck," *Policy Review*, Summer 1991. See also the essay by Czechoslovakia's Finance Minister, Vaclav Klaus, *Dismantling Socialism: A Preliminary Report* (Sydney, Australia: The Centre for Independent Studies,

1991). Klaus provides a clear statement of the determined, and highly successful, manner in which he has been leading his country to freedom.

8. An essay on this subject by Josef Zverina—which he dedicates "To my friends and enemies"—is graphically titled "On Not Living in Hatred"; it appears in Havel et al., *The Power of the Powerless*, pp. 207-16.

9. *Ibid.*, p. 212.

10. See, for example, the well-documented book by Janice Broun, *Conscience and Captivity: Religion in Eastern Europe* (Washington: Ethics and Public Policy Center, 1988), which illustrates the extraordinary survival of religion under Communism despite great odds throughout East-Central Europe.

11. Dobbs, "Nationalism Replacing Communism" (see n. 1 above), p. A32.

12. Vladimir Tismaneanu, "The Ambiguity of Romanian National Communism," *Telos*, no. 60 (Summer 1984), p. 70.

13. Cited in Dobbs, "Nationalism Replacing Communism," p. A32.

14. Quoted in Mary Battiata, "Ethnic Politics Returns to Bulgaria," *The Washington Post*, October 27, 1991, p. A32.

15. Zlatko Anguelov, "Nationalism and Pseudo-Nationalism," *East European Reporter*, vol. 4, no. 4 (Summer 1991), p. 41.

16. Walter Kolarz, *Myths and Realities in Eastern Europe* (London: Lindsay Drummond Ltd., 1946), pp. 13-14.

17. Oscar Janowsky, *Nationalities and National Minorities (With Special Reference to East-Central Europe)* (New York: Macmillan, 1945), p. 20.

18. Isaiah Berlin, *The Crooked Timber of Humanity* (see introduction, n. 2 above), p. 245.

19. Kohn, *The Idea of Nationalism* (see ch. 1, n. 18 above), p. 329.

20. *Ibid.*, p. 330.

21. Peter F. Sugar and Ivo Lederer, eds., *Nationalism in Eastern Europe* (Seattle & London: University of Washington Press, 1969), p. 11.

22. Johann Gottfried von Herder, *Sammtliche Werke* (see ch. 1, n. 12 above), vol. 1, pp. 283, 676.

23. *Ibid.*, p. 669.

24. Cited in Hans Kohn, *Pan-Slavism, Its History and Ideology* (New York: Vintage Russian Library, 1960), p. 9.

25. Kohn, *Nationalism: Its Meaning and History* (see ch. 1, n. 11 above), p. 46.

26. *Ibid.*, pp. 48-49.

27. Ivan Volgyes, "Legitimacy and Modernization," in *The Politics of Ethnicity in Eastern Europe*, ed. George Klein and Milan J. Reban (New York: Columbia University Press, 1981), p. 133.

28. Sugar, "Problems of Nationalism in Eastern Europe" (see ch. 1, n. 44 above), p. 7.

29. R. V. Burks, *The Dynamics of Communism in Eastern Europe* (Princeton: Princeton University Press, 1961), p. 188.

30. Klein and Reban, introduction to *The Politics of Ethnicity in Eastern Europe* (see n. 27 above), p. 3.

Chapter III

1. Stephen Fischer-Galati, "Romanian Nationalism," in *Nationalism in Eastern Europe* (see ch. 2, n. 21 above), p. 374.

2. Georgescu saw flickers of national self-consciousness as early as 1478 in Stephen the Great, who twice in a single document used the phrase "the other Romanian country" for Wallachia. Sixteenth-century chronicles commonly describe events in both provinces; a Wallachian printer dedicated the books he published in Transylvania to "all Romanian brothers," and a group of Wallachian boyars proposed a political collaboration with Moldavia in 1599 since "we are all of one creed and one language." See Vlad Georgescu, *The Romanians: A History* (Columbus: Ohio State University Press, 1991), p. 70.

3. *Ibid.*, p. 71.

4. Keith Hitchins, *Studies on Romanian National Consciousness* (Pelham N.Y.: Nagard Publisher, 1983), p. 13.

5. *Ibid.*, pp. 48-50.

6. See, for example, Radu Pantazi, *Simion Barnutiu-Opere si Gandirea* (Bucharest, 1924), pp. 119-252.

7. C. A. Rosetti, "Catre Fratii Nostri din Moldova," in *Pruncul Roman*, 1848, VI. 12, no. 1.

8. Georgescu notes that in the 1840s there was a passion for history, which was used in political arguments as a justification for nationalism. See *The Romanians*, p. 142.

9. Ion C. Bratianu, "Programul Romanului," in *Romanul*, 1857, VIII. 9, no. 1.

10. *Ibid.*

11. Andras Keszthelyi, "The Ideological Peculiarities of Romanian Liberalism," unpublished.

12. *Ibid.*

13. *Minority Rights: Problems, Parameters, and Patterns in the CSCE Context* (Washington: Commission on Security and Cooperation in Europe, 1991), p. 148.

14. For more on the historical background of the current Hungarian-Romanian conflict, see *Destroying Ethnic Identity: The Hungarians of Romania* (Helsinki Watch Report, February 1989).

15. Georgescu, *The Romanians* (see n. 2 above), pp. 165-66.

16. Laszlo Kurti, "Transylvania, Land Beyond Reason: Toward an Anthropological Analysis of a Contested Terrain," *Dialectical Anthropology*, vol. 14 (1989), pp. 21-52. Kurti provides a very useful discussion of the background of the Hungarian-Romanian conflict.

17. Georgescu adds, however, that virtually no new conceptual innovations to the concept of Romanian nationalism were added in the nineteenth century. See *The Romanians*, p. 181.

18. Kurti, "Transylvania, Land Beyond Reason," p. 28.

19. Wesley Marxh Gewehr, *The Rise of Nationalism in the Balkans, 1800-1930* (Hamden, Conn.: Archon Books, 1967), p. 67.

20. Thus Seymour Cain points out that the Guard's manifestations of anti-Semitism "are regarded as betrayals of the essentially non-violent, sacrifician teachings of Codreanu." See Cain's "Mircea Eliade, the Iron Guard, and Romanian Anti-Semitism," *Midstream*, vol. 35, no. 8 (November 1989).

21. Virgil Nemoianu, "Development Models and Social Value Choices in the Rumanian 1940's: The Case of *Cercul Literar* in Sibiu,"

International Journal of Rumanian Studies, vol. 7, no. 1a (1989), p. 55.

22. *Ibid.,* p. 56.

23. Fischer-Galati, "Romanian Nationalism" in *Nationalism in Eastern Europe* (see ch. 2, n. 21 above), p. 394.

24. "The illegal Romanian Communist Party was dominated by Transylvanians and Bessarabians, whose political radicalization had been facilitated by the local revolutionary traditions and patterns." Vladimir Tismaneanu, "Understanding National Stalinism: Romanian Communism in a Historical-Comparative Perspective," in *Analele Universitatii Bucuresti: Istorie* (Bucharest, 1990), p. 29.

25. Dorin Tudoran, *Romania: A Case of Dynastic Communism* (New York: Freedom House, 1989), p. 18.

26. Vladimir Tismaneanu, "Understanding National Stalinism: A Comparative Approach to the History of Romanian Communism," Occasional Paper Number 25 (Washington: Woodrow Wilson Center, 1990), p. 3.

27. Georgescu, *The Romanians* (see n. 2 above), p. 273.

28. Tismaneanu, "Understanding National Stalinism," p. 31.

29. On the issue of nationalism as a legitimizing tool in that period, see (in addition to the many writings of Vladimir Tismaneanu) Robert R. King, *A History of the Romanian Communist Party* (Stanford: Hoover Institution Press, 1980); and George Schopflin, "Romanian Nationalism," *Survey,* vol. 20, nos. 2-3 (1978), pp. 77-104.

30. See Edward Behr, *Kiss the Hand You Cannot Bite: The Rise and Fall of the Ceausescus* (New York: Villard Books, 1991), p. 146. This statement, incidentally, is simply incorrect: Shakespeare was consistently shown on the Romanian stage throughout the Dej and Ceausescu years, and surely Handel could be heard on Romanian national radio.

31. See Ion Mihai Pacepa, *Red Horizons: Chronicles of a Communist Spy Chief* (Washington: Regnery/Gateway, 1987) for a chilling account of Ceausescu's terror network.

32. Robert R. King, *Minorities Under Communism: Nationalities as a Source of Tension among Balkan Communist States* (Cambridge: Harvard University Press, 1973), p. 153.

33. See "Hungarians in Romania," in *Minority Rights: Problems,*

Parameters, and Patterns in the CSCE Context (Washington: Commission on Security and Cooperation in Europe, 1991), p. 150.

34. See, for example, *Destroying Ethnic Identity: The Hungarians of Romania* (Helsinki Watch Report, February 1989).

35. Katherine Verdery, "Romanian Identity and Cultural Politics Under Ceausescu: An Example from Philosophy," Occasional Paper Number 17 (Washington: Woodrow Wilson Center, 1989), p. 9.

36. See Virgil Nemoianu, "Mihai Sora and the Traditions of Romanian Philosophy," *The Review of Metaphysics*, vol. 43 (March 1990), pp. 591-605.

37. Dennis Deletant, "The Role of Vatra Romaneasca in Transylvania," *Radio Free Europe: Report on Eastern Europe*, February 1, 1991, p. 29.

38. Adela Becleanu Iancu, "Elemente de Filosofie Nescrisa in Cultura Romaneasca," *Romania Literara*, vol. 21 (June 23, 1988), p. 19.

39. Verdery, "Romanian Identity," p. 21.

40. Cited in Michael Shafir, "Schopflinian Realism and Romanian Reality," *Radio Free Europe: Report on Eastern Europe*, February 15, 1991, p. 35.

41. Andrei Cornea, "Old Scenarios, New Actors" *22*, no. 26 (July 13, 1990).

42. There is no precise translation for "mare"—it means both "great" and "large," ambiguously—thus making both a cultural and a territorial point at the same time.

43. See Shafir, "Schopflinian Realism and Romanian Reality," p. 40. The Italian courts decided on November 30, 1990, that the charge printed in the Italian publication *Panorama*—that the émigré in question, Dragan, was a "fascist, legionaire, and a collaborationist of the Ceausescu regime"—was factual. See *Romania Libera,* December 4, 1990.

44. Nestor Ratesh, *Romania: The Entangled Revolution* (Washington: Center for Strategic and International Studies, 1991), p. 143.

45. Michael Shafir, "The Greater Romania Party," *Radio Free Europe: Report on Eastern Europe*, November 15, 1991, p. 26.

46. *Ibid.*, p. 27.

47. On Cornea, see *Dimineata*, August 4, 1990; and on Ratiu, see *Azi*, July 25, 1990.

48. "International Protection of National Minorities—An Imperative for the Hungarians of Rumania," Memorandum for the Copenhagen Meeting on the Human Dimension of the CSCE, June 5-29, 1990, by the Hungarian Human Rights Foundation.

49. A clear taxonomy may be found in Roger Pilon, "Ordering Rights Consistently: Or What We Do and Do Not Have Rights To," *The Georgia Law Review*, vol. 13, no. 4 (Summer 1979), pp. 1171-96.

50. For a good summary of the Gypsy situation, see Dan Ionescu, "The Gypsies Organize," *Radio Free Europe: Report on Eastern Europe*, June 29, 1990, pp. 39-42.

51. Nicolae Manolescu, "Tribal Democracy and Liberal Democracy," *Romania Literara*, vol. 45 (November 7, 1991), p. 2.

52. Gheorghe Serban, "Timisoara Is Different," *Uncaptive Minds*, Spring 1991, p. 39.

53. Vasile Popovici, "Societatile Din Subterana" (Subterranean Societies), *Meridian*, vol. 1, no. 4 (November-December 1991). See the Afterword for complete text.

Chapter IV

1. John Locke, *The Second Treatise on Civil Government* (Indianapolis, New York: Bobbs-Merrill, 1952), ch. 6, par. 57, p. 32.

2. *Ibid.*, ch. 15, par. 171, p. 97.

3. *Selected Writings of John Stuart Mill*, ed. Maurice Cowling (New York and Toronto: New American Library, 1968), p. 172.

4. Henry M. Brackenridge, "A Vindication of Civil Rights for Jews," in *Annals of America* (Chicago, London: Encyclopaedia Britannica, Inc., 1968), vol. 4, p. 559.

5. Mill, *Selected Writings*, p. 178.

6. Ludwig von Mises, *Nation, State, and Economy: Contributions to the Politics and History of Our Time* (New York and London: New York University Press, 1983), pp. 10-11.

7. *Ibid.*, p. 35.

8. *Ibid.*, p. 34.

9. *Ibid.*, p. 36.

10. *Ibid.*

11. *Ibid.*, p. 49.

12. *Ibid.*, p. 51.

13. *Ibid.*, p. 96.

14. For a brief look at Hayek's considerable influence on dissident thought in East-Central Europe, see Juliana Geran Pilon, "A Great Man—and a Great Idea," *The Wall Street Journal*, November 18, 1991.

15. Friedrich A. Hayek, *The Road to Serfdom* (Chicago: University of Chicago Press, 1944), ch. 10, p. 140.

16. *Ibid.*, p. 144.

17. Cited in Kolarz, *Myths and Realities* (see ch. 2, n. 16 above), p. 98.

Index

About the Author

Juliana Geran Pilon is the Director of Programs for the Americas, Asia, and Europe at the International Foundation for Electoral Systems in Washington, D.C., which offers assistance to the democratic electoral infrastructure throughout the world. She also teaches the history of ideas at Johns Hopkins University and at American University. Born in Romania, she came to the United States with her family as a teenager after their seventeen-year attempt to emigrate, receiving her doctorate in philosophy from the University of Chicago as a Danforth Fellow and a Woodrow Wilson Fellow. Dr. Pilon has since taught at several universities, including Emory University, the University of Chicago, and California State University, having held post-doctoral fellowships at Stanford University's Hoover Institution on War, Revolution, and Peace, and at the Institute for Humane Studies. In 1981, she was named Senior Policy Analyst at one of Washington's most influential research institutes, the Heritage Foundation. From 1988 until 1991, she was the Executive Director, and then Vice President, of the National Forum Foundation, where she helped establish the most extensive internship program for Eastern Europeans in the United States.

The author of over 150 articles, reviews, and monographs, Dr. Pilon has published in *The Wall Street Journal, The New*

York Times, National Review, Commentary, The National Interest, and many other publications in the United States and abroad. She has appeared often on national television and radio, and speaks frequently before civic and university audiences. Her autobiographical book, *Notes From the Other Side of Night,* originally published in 1979 in the United States, is scheduled for publication in Romania in early 1992.